MW01001147

# Space and Learning
# Lessons in Architecture 3

Herman Hertzberger

010 Publishers, Rotterdam 2008

# Piet Mondrian, Victory Boogie Woogie, 1942-1944

Space as handled by Mondrian, perfectly expressed in this painting, is equally a model for what architects could do when making space so that it leaves room for a wealth of changing activities and the wealth of relational situations these entail.

*Victory Boogie Woogie* bids farewell to the old world where things unequivocally are what they are and stay that way. Its patches of colour are in motion whilst standing still, and as they seemingly shift it is as if they have been placed at random, as if they have no fixed place and don't really belong anywhere. The painting is not at rest, it is a rest in unrest. All its components are in an unstable equilibrium that looks as though it might collapse at any moment.

Nor is there any sense of hierarchy. All parts are interchangeable without upsetting the equilibrium. A multi-centrality prevails – that is, many centres are feasible, without letting go of the painting's principles. In fact each part could be a centre but it could also be in-between space. In other words, main issues can just as easily become side issues and vice versa; it all depends on how you look at it. To compound matters, the painting is unfinished; what we see is a stage in a process that could easily have continued. Nothing definitive then, just a moment in time.

[1] Piet Mondrian, 1872-1944
*Victory Boogie Woogie*
(unfinished) 1944
Oils and paper on canvas
Diagonal, 178.4 cm
©2008 Mondriaan/Holtzman Trust
c/o HCR International Virginia USA

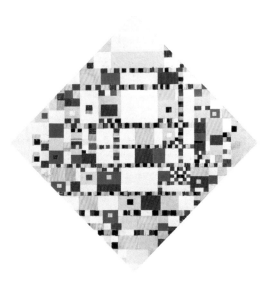

[1]

# Preface

This book is about architecture and education and at the same time it is not. The title, *Space and Learning*, intimates that it is about what lies *between* architecture and education and how the two, given certain conditions, influence one another. It is those conditions that are uppermost in these pages. Rather than being a litany of successful projects, it seeks to show how space can be a stimulus to learning.

As an architect, it is impossible to avoid largely proceeding from your own work and using it as research material. And this is very much the case here. Material from elsewhere served me as a source of inspiration or to confirm my own conclusions.

As work on the book proceeded, its format grew almost unobserved in the direction of two preceding books, *Lessons for Students in Architecture 1 (Making Space, Leaving Space)* and *Space and the Architect (Lessons in Architecture 2)*. So *Space and Learning* became part three of the series.

Space and learning… not being told how it should be done, but, in the words of Maria Montessori, learning to do it yourself. This then is the principal objective of schools: learning to learn. *Space and Learning* describes how the space for learning can meet this objective.

I would like to thank all those who contributed with such dedication to seeing this book through publication: publisher Hans Oldewarris, Piet Gerards and Maud van Rossum for the book design, Veroon Hertzberger for reading through the draft version and her remarks on educationalism, Marieke Schalkwijk, Tim Loeters, Ellen Haverkate and Erik de Jong for the drawings and diagrams, Pia Elia as secretary and documentalist, Jop Voorn for the text research, Eva de Bruijn for the picture editing and Vibeke Gieskes for the text editing and image research.

Herman Hertzberger
August 2008

# 4
# The City as a Macro-School | 202

# Foreword

Think of schools and usually it still conjures up visions of classrooms with blackboards and teachers up front doing their best to make the children facing them a little wiser. Throughout the world, particularly in economically distressed areas where children still manage to go to school, they eagerly absorb everything taught them. They know all too well that only learning can free them from their predicament and give them the prospect of a better life. In most of the world though, there is simply not the means to achieve even the most basic physical conditions for education: four walls, some openings to let in light, a roof…

Elsewhere, it is a place where pupils are more demanding and learning has to be more than just absorbing basic knowledge. In the relatively affluent countries with their increasing dependence on knowledge, the claims on space are getting greater too. Indeed, in the knowledge society differentiation is on the increase and with it comes the need for smaller working groups. Not just that, school equipment is getting more and more expensive. So the means necessary to achieve these more elevated objectives are often themselves unforthcoming. Moreover, the proportionately increasing onus on the profession of teacher has been grossly miscalculated, resulting in an ever greater scarcity of decent teachers. This shortage worldwide is expected to get worse and if only for that reason new forms of learning will require new spatial conditions alongside the traditional teacher-fronted lessons.

And as the interest in more individual-based education continues to increase, so does the spatial complexity of school buildings. Working alone or in groups requires more and more workplaces, though without endangering the view of the whole. This overall view is necessary as a support to the teaching staff, but also for helping pupils to find their bearings in the welter of options open to them.

The school must be an ever-changing, stimulating environment where there is a lot going on and there are choices to be made, as in a shop where everything is laid out waiting for you. Not only that, children have to contend with other children; they learn to do things together, take another into account, work things out between them,

[1]

understand each other. This is a great deal more than reading, writing and arithmetic and the school space must encourage it.

Young and less-young children are confronted with all these new phenomena in what is for them a new environment and community – in effect a model of a city-in-miniature and thus a potted version of the world; the world in a nutshell.

Not only does the school become like a city; with learning expanding beyond the school curriculum it is important that our entire environment is educational. Just as continuing education (*éducation permanente*) is no longer confined to school hours, so with learning leaving the school territory and embracing the surroundings as a whole we can speak of 'boundless education'. Then not only does the school become a small city but the city becomes an exceedingly large school. This is a call to make the city instructive, a 'Learning City', in other words a stimulating, meaningful environment that points people, especially young people, in the right direction and leaves them wiser.

Add to that the fact that psychologists and psychiatrists keep harping on about the considerable influence the surroundings have on children of school age and that the first conscious impressions of one's surroundings are decisive for the rest of your life, for your sense of quality and for what you expect of life. So it is important that those surroundings are as rich and varied as can be, evoking as many positive associations as possible and leaving the best of memories. The things you recall best of your own school are the classrooms, the corridors, the stairs, the windows you looked out through, the space, the materials and perhaps the attic full of old stuff where you had no business being. Then there are the others – much like you but different – the friendships, the crushes and, in terms of schoolwork, what you were praised for or, alternatively, what earned you black marks.

Do those who found schools, finance them, design them, build them, fit them out, take account of all this in their programme and realize the responsibility they are taking on?

Architects who design schools have to do more than provide routine tricks and good-looking run-of-the-mill solutions. What schools really need – anything designed in fact – is a precision in the conditions they are offering. Just as we see learning as second nature and an enlargement of one's space, it should be second nature to architects to prime space to those ends.

[2]

# Architecture and Schools

Architecture has unfailingly approached the designing of schools from a less than critical position. All the while, it seems, architects meekly followed their briefs and were mainly concerned with formal aspects of the exterior without busying themselves with spatial opportunities that might lead to better education, and with the role they themselves might fulfil there.

There can be few building types that have so poorly evolved during the past hundred years as schools. It was only in the closing decade of the 20th century that we saw deviations from a type that has been standard since the year dot. Only the form, particularly that of the exterior, moved with the times. How schools were organized was evidently unassailable.

There have been many admirable schools designed in the 20th century by architects of wide-ranging persuasion, schools distinguished in terms of materials and fenestration with rows of rectangular classrooms off long corridors. Not that we can find much fault in the 'architecture', their exteriors; on the contrary, relatively many monumental

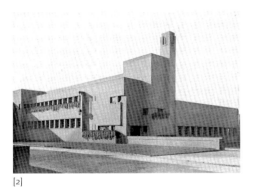

[2]

[4]

[6]

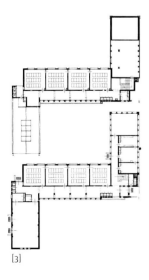

[3]

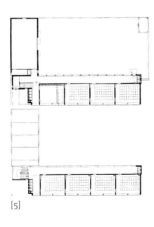

[5]

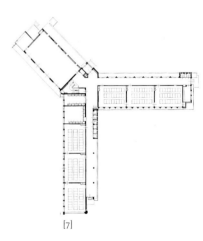

[7]

[1]

[3]

[2]

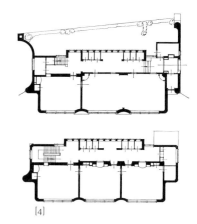

[4]

schools, excessively so at times, have been built and these often managed to upgrade their surroundings.

In the Netherlands of the 1920s and '30s the local Public Works departments strove to give schools, a genre particularly well-represented on their agenda, a distinct countenance. With this, they sought to draw attention both contextually and architecturally to the key position they intended for education. The schools built in Hilversum, designed by W.M. Dudok in his capacity of City Architect, became particularly celebrated. But the many instigated and drafted by Public Works in Amsterdam to designs by the lesser-known second generation of Amsterdam School architects, amongst whom A.R. Hulshoff, N. Lansdorp, P.L. Marnette and A.J. Westerman, likewise established schools as a building type. These distinctive, elongated buildings underlined by the horizontal disposition of their windows and punctuated by monumental stair towers, were often striking cornerstones in what were then the newer residential areas. They were soon regarded as the 'churches' of these new districts, culturally as well as contextually. Evidently, this additional prestige spoke louder than the clamour that is part and parcel of schools and difficult to avoid.

A striking aspect was the consistency in form and materials but even more so the elongated floor plans with classrooms almost invariably on one side, the side facing the sun. This criterion effectively ruled out the possibility of a type with classrooms on two sides of a central corridor and so gave rise to the principle of two architecturally distinct sides, the front and the rear. The classrooms were usually glazed to the hilt on the inner side of the block, with a relatively closed, more monumentally inclined facade on the corridor side. With the playground on the sunward side, preferably as part of the block's inner courtyard, the school invariably showed its stern monumental side to the street.

And so the school building became a type, readily identifiable and familiar in the cityscape and fully integrated and assimilated in the urban blocks. Indeed, these schools expressed in their monumentality and not without pride the unconditional acceptance of educational institutions in the social democracy of the first half of the 20th century.

These days, as it happens, we are back to classrooms facing the sun. With perimeter blocks becoming a thing of the past, the typical school building disappeared and schools as free-standing entities arrived on the scene. Formal frames of reference, usually imposed by the local government inspectors, such as the orientation of classrooms, continued to dominate the designs.

There is no better example of architecture seen as largely a question of exteriors than schools. Their internal arrangement has always been the same: classrooms as opaque boxes off long straight corridors purely for circulation and for hanging coats. And though new ideas on education emerged, unrelievedly calling for greater independence among pupils and expressing increasing doubt about traditional teacher-fronted lessons, these never resulted in breaking down the classroom as a self-contained bastion. It would seem that the inexorable spatial consequence of more independence among pupils, of opening up the classroom, never really got as far as the architecture.

It is striking that even modern architecture scarcely responded to this development, though this 'heroic' style professed to be the face of social reform. Modernist architects were most concerned instead with larger windows and greater transparency, chiefly oriented to the world outside.

Open-air schools were popular among architects, probably because they were an excuse for using masses of glass, but they brought no change to the authoritarian proportions of time-honoured orthodox education. Clearly, architects however progressive were simply not concerned with renewal in teaching and learning. Thus, if we look beyond the magnificent glass expanses in Duiker's Open-Air School, we see children still sitting on traditional school benches, although these were designed anew and are sometimes used in the open air, weather permitting.

The only ground-breaking element, besides the hygiene aspect, is the view, though this is grievously restricted here by the nearby block of houses surrounding the school, not least so that those living there can easily look into the building. A serious response to the new much-discussed new pedagogical insights, however, is nowhere to be seen.

This celebrated Open-Air School (1929-1930) by J. Duiker may be spectacular in its transparency and its marvellously pure construction, but in fact it is a version, opened

[5]

[6]

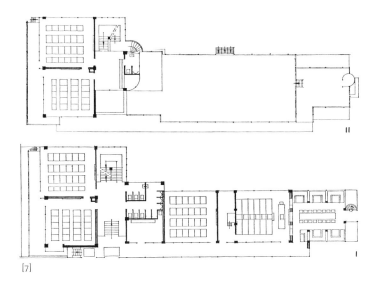

[7]

[8]

up to the outside, of the traditional classroom system in which children, all that light and air notwithstanding, are still taught along traditional lines. The corridors are actually widened landings of the main stair containing nothing but pegs hung with coats. Even here, you could be sent out into the corridor, in full view of the residents of the surrounding block and looking even more pathetic. Conversely, this fuelled the voyeurism of the children, who are all too willingly distracted by the view into the houses so close by. This demonstrative extroversion leads more to a trivial view out than a truly 'functional' one.

[1]

What mattered to Duiker is made clear in his description of the Open-Air School, whose title translates as 'A healthy school for the healthy child':
"It is a vigorously hygienic force that influences our lives and will grow into a style – a hygienic style! The one-sided emphasis placed on training the mind, as 'scholastic dogma', hampers the necessary attention from being devoted to bodily powers and potentials present in nascent form in the child. Yet the normal development of the mind is bound to a normal development of the body.
"Banished between four walls in overfull classes, bound for hours on end to subject matter that is often not understood, often into the evening in poor light, under more or less rigid discipline – this is how children spend their young lives of joy and gaiety. That which the adult casts off when not coerced by necessity and life's cares, is what the child must bear.
"There are of course the newer pedagogical methods: the Montessori and Dalton systems, each of which makes its own special demands on dimensions and division of the schoolroom. These are most certainly of the greatest importance for the child. But these pedagogic systems are not as influential on the architecture of the school building as the hygienic factor of 'immaterializing' the structure, which has a much more general character. This, then, is the stepping-off point for our philosophy of modern school-building. As long as the school remains the school for healthy children, the way the home until now has been the home for heathy people – that is, both lagging hopelessly behind in our recent hygienic world view – the younger generation in its strong tendency towards bodily culture will have to clear them out and modernize them."[1]

[2]

For Duiker the emphasis was on how architecture could contribute to hygiene as the condition for bodily well-being. In this he saw a legitimation of his quest for purity and a directness of form, in other words without ribs and ridges, corners, gaps and other potential gatherers of dust and bacteria. To get rid of dust though dematerialization and lightness – as much in the sense of construction as in that of creating spaces of maximum daylight – for him stood for a better and healthier world. Development of the mind came second. It is safe to assume that here Duiker is expressing the ideas of his generation of modernist architects, a generation that was simply not concerned with the spatial consequences of renewal in education.

[3]

Presumably the education side was not exactly being pressurized to emerge with new paradigms of spatial order either. The idea of an open-air school was new in itself and was meant for every child, "for the *healthy* child", and so not just for the physically impaired as was originally intended.
Be that as it may, this development had not the slightest implications for education as such and even less for designing schools. It did cause the emphasis to come to lie on

[1, 2] J. Duiker, Open-Air School, Cliostraat, Amsterdam, 1929-1930

[3] H.B. van Broekhuizen, Arnhemse Buitenschool Monniken-huizen, Arnhem, 1930

[4] Lessons among the dunes, Scheveningen

[5] Outdoor classroom, Katwijk (photo Ed van Wijk)

balconies, terraces and loggias, which were eagerly seized upon by architects to sculpturally embellish the outsides of their school buildings.

This drawing-in of the outside world, however wonderfully done, remained limited to a largely physical experience through the assumed beneficial effects of sun and air on the pupils' bodily and mental condition.

Again, the open-air school phenomenon as the ultimate mix of inside and outside failed to bring about a new attitude to nature, let alone to the outside world socially, as one would expect. Even so-called outdoor classrooms were in fact only indoor classrooms moved or placed outside, and functioning exactly as they did inside. In psychological terms this may have worked as something of a 'liberation of the surrounding wall', yet in fact it only meant more distraction and inconvenience through gusts of wind and raindrops that could unexpectedly disturb the concentration. Indeed, it probably was additionally frustrating to have to sit still and absorb the day-to-day subject matter with so much around to incite one's interest and curiosity.

The open-air school radiates freedom above all else, liberation from the customary heavy brick and stone buildings. Glazed walls bring transparency, views out and in. These glass schools therefore offered first and foremost a preview of a new, more open world where teaching and learning are integrated along more natural lines – despite the vicissitudes of the weather, which could meanwhile be countered by such technical resources as anti-sun glass and double glazing.

Designed by architects of the Modern Movement, these schools may have done nothing to change the way schools were traditionally organized but they did replace the school building as a bastion of severity and gravity with an image of openness and accessibility that attested, outwardly at least, to a new spirit in education.

Their architects sought to make outer walls for the classrooms that could be slid or folded away to let in the outside world. Arnhemse Buitenschool (1930) designed by H.B. van Broekhuizen was a convincing and extremely early example (though it seems to have been suggested to its architect by an English example from 1924 in Uffculme by Cossins, Peacock & Belway).

[4]

[5]

So the Heroic Period may have produced few if any school buildings with revolutionary spatial concepts that influenced ideas on learning, but it did forge the spatial tools for today's schools, oriented to the outside world but above all opened up inwards. Transparency and an open arrangement are now second nature, and have undoubtedly helped to shape the image of space in the modern school.

In the 1930s, the services of architects were enlisted by socialist administrators to generate with their new architecture images expressing the social reforms these had in mind. Primarily this meant educational facilities. This led to large well-lit structures with masses of space, such as André Lurçat's Karl Marx School complex (1931-1933) in

[1-4] H.B. van Broekhuizen, Arnhemse Buitenschool Monniken-huizen, Arnhem, 1930

[5, 6] Cossins, Peacock & Belway, Open-Air School, Uffculme, England, 1924

[7-9] André Lurçat, Karl Marx School, Villejuif, Paris, 1931-1933

[1]

[2]

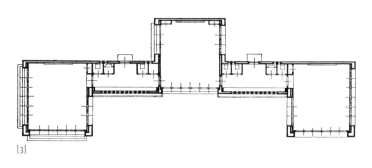

[3]

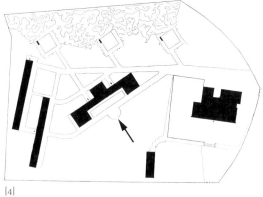

[4]

[5]

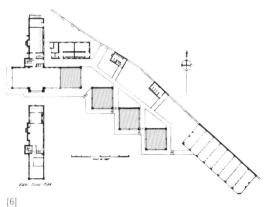

[6]

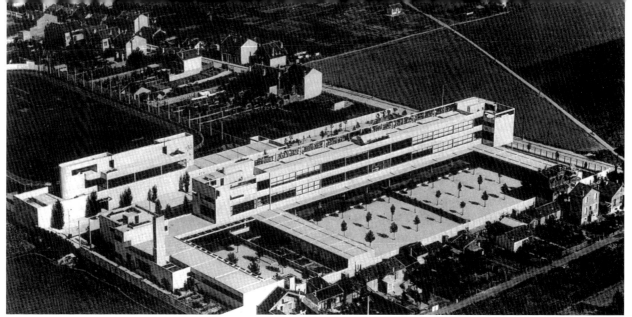

[7]

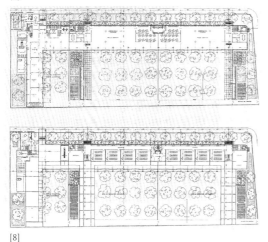

[8]

[9]

Villejuif south of Paris. Although the floor plans give the impression that the teaching there was still entirely traditional in conception, the school was certainly imbued with a new spirit.

An exceptionally innovative example at the time was Beaudoin and Lods' Open-Air School in Suresnes (1935-1936), which was more like a settlement than a building, particularly in its layout. A typical feature, indeed for open-air schools in general, was the strong attention to the outdoor spaces.

Most striking are the ingenious accordion partitions which virtually left the classrooms outside. With classrooms sited singly as if free-standing houses, it was almost inevitable that classes would gain a greater sense of independence and of the distinction between them. Emphasis was on the facilities on offer, amongst them accommodation for dining, afternoon naps (with an option on outdoors) and physical training.

"The school was regarded as an institute, in this case set up by a progressive-minded local councillor, that besides imparting knowledge was also and more importantly to bring the physical condition of particularly the weaker pupils up to scratch. Thus the school gained an aspect of welfare. This new paradigm was of course an imposed condition and even a necessity for creating a wholly new conception of schools in which emphasis came to lie on collective facilities such as washrooms, dining rooms and restrooms."[2]

[1]

[2]

[3]

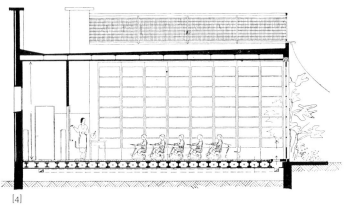

[4]

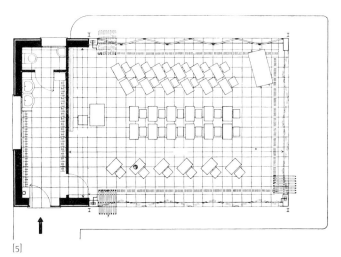

[5]

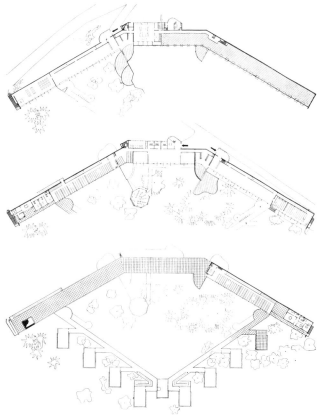

[6]

[7]

[8]

The new transparent and radiant schools that emerged in the 1920s and '30s as testimony to a better world, established a new image of hygiene, health, more space, openness, light, air and views.

Architects took their inspiration from the assumed link between air, light and health. The immediate consequences were visible in the exteriors of the new generation of buildings. As for the interiors, the main focus was now on quantitative criteria entirely appropriate to the rationalist component of Modern Movement architecture such as sanitation, sufficient light, ventilation and heating; influences of the more toned-down approach that in the early 1930s had produced new departure-points tailor-made for the Modern architects. These aspects were undoubtedly useful and necessary for the development of school-building. There was no sign as yet of the bureaucratic standards that would breed here and much later systematically and ruthlessly suppress all the freedom there had been.

Perhaps it was Hannes Meyer who first took these aspects as a stepping-off point in the 1926 competition design he made with Hans Jakob Wittwer for the Peterschule in Basle.

"The issues that preoccupied him were the more down-to-earth ones like good lighting in the classrooms, and he may perhaps have been the first to call for a more scientific approach and objectivity in school architecture. It is interesting, then, how this show of unquestioning faith in the potential of modern technology should so spectacularly, and for us inexplicably, overshoot the mark in economic terms."[3]

Evidently the concepts of other forms of education failed to resonate sufficiently to set architects thinking and set them to work. Or was a new design made to the old familiar ordering principles more than enough to keep them busy?

It is only in schools specially built for a particular type of innovative education – Montessori schools, for instance, a great many of which were built in Amsterdam by Public Works – that we find modifications to the traditional arrangement of space. But these are exceptions that failed to get themselves accepted as a new type. One obvious reason was that the financing authorities were sceptical and afraid of getting involved with fly-by-night experiments. Hence the continued prevalence of the most general-purpose school type, in other words the time-honoured rectangular, unarticulated classrooms. However new, and however much imbued with the spirit of idealism of those days, this architecture failed to alter the essential relationships in schools and education. As almost always, it was a trend-follower instead of a trendsetter, even though architecture is the pre-eminent instrument to make that other paradigm happen, certainly in

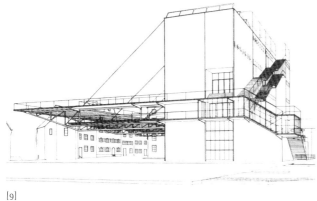

[9]

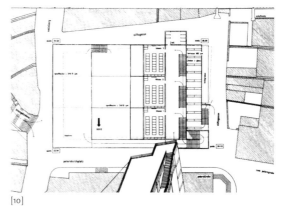

[10]

education and most specifically where the social relations of teaching and learning are concerned. It is just such an evolution in education involving increased freedom for pupils that necessitates alternatives for walls and doors, and thus a change of tack in the thinking on spatial conditions. If there is one area where making space presents a special challenge for architecture, it is in designing schools.

[1]

The schools built between 1944 and 1960 in the English county of Hertfordshire commanded attention less through the new forms of space for education than through the élan displayed by the government in tackling the shortage brought about by the war. Using industrially produced, standardized light steel members relatively cheap results could be quickly achieved with a surprising freedom in how the floor plans were organized. In this respect the restrictions on space imposed by the rectangular format of the construction could have been a lot worse. For example, small shifts effected between what were uninspiring classrooms produced surprisingly useful corridor spaces. The real problem resides in the distressingly thin, even spindly results that recall little of an environment of instruction. There is nothing wrong with projecting an industrial mood, but the bare steel components and panels here are too light and bony, whereas other buildings from that time – such as the Eames House in Los Angeles, itself assembled from industrial elements – show that an inspirational layout and cladding are eminently feasible.

[2]

What is interesting is the discussion that broke out in the wake of the Smithsons' criticism of these steel prefab schools prompted by their Hunstanton School of 1949-1954, which for the record perhaps has something of a factory itself but was architecturally stronger and of a more tectonic and severe design. In 1953 the Smithsons claimed that besides "an everyday life of teaching children" there must also be "a secret life of pure space, the permanent built Form … which will continue to exist as idea".* Countermanding this is the critique of the Young Fabian Socialists in their pamphlet "Architecture: Art or Service" (1963), in which Hunstanton was criticized "for being nothing but art, whereas the schools of Hertfordshire were 'teaching buildings, not architectonic monuments'."[4]

[3]

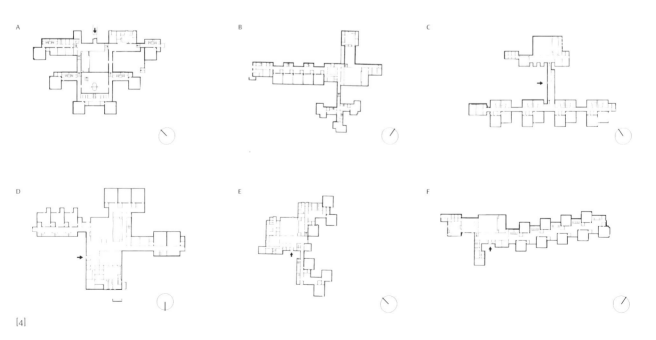
[4]

This discussion exposes architecture's two-faced stance towards the designing of schools. By this is meant the wedge driven between those organizations geared to education (and teaching) and architecture, as though it were a choice between alternatives, one a question of fitness for purpose and the other a free-ranging idea hovering above it. There is only one kind of architecture, however: an architecture that must make space for education (in other words teaching and learning) and even incite such space-making. What may be expected of the space that constitutes a school and what conditions can be achieved within the domain of architecture? That is what this book is all about.

1  From J. Duiker, "Een gezonde school voor het gezonde kind", *de 8 en Opbouw*, 1932, pp. 88-92 (trans. JK)
2  *Lessons 2*, p. 55
3  *Lessons 2*, p. 68
4  Ariane Wilson, "Form et programme: le cas des écoles Anglaises après guèrre", in *l'Architecture d'Aujourd'hui*, no. 339, March-April 2002, p. 97

[*] *"We must answer the functional requirements of the moment in such a way that the resulting built form has a permanent validity. "Tomorrow will inherit only space Our ultimate responsibility is therefore the creation of noble space. Consider, therefore, the Hunstanton School as having two lives: an everyday life of teaching children, noise, furniture, and chalk dust, as equals with the building elements, all of which add up the word 'School'. And a secret life of pure space, the permanent built Form which will persist when School has given way to Museum or Warehouse, and which will continue to exist as idea even when the Built Form has long disappeared. It is through built form that the inherent nobility of man finds release."*

Peter Smithson, 1954, in: 'Reflections on Hunstanton Becoming a School'

[5]

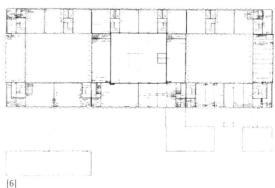

[6]

# 1  The Classroom Dethroned

## The classroom as private domain

Classrooms have traditionally been the principal building stones of schools. All over the world, children have been brought together in classrooms since the earliest times. The teacher at the blackboard passes on knowledge. So the spatial conditions of the classrooms should mainly serve to aid the pupils' concentration, which should be distracted as little as possible, while the teacher should have the best possible overview. Indeed, classrooms have always been the explicit domain of the teacher, and pupils are either lucky or unlucky with the one they get.

The basic principle behind the physical make-up of schools was and still is a series of autonomous spaces separated from each other and reached from often long corridors through doors set without exception at the side of the teacher and blackboard and usually with a window so high up that only the teachers are in a position to look in and out through it.

It was only in the second half of the 20th century that this archetype of the classroom as basic pedagogical space unit was opened up bit by bit, influenced by innovative ideas on education. So the time-honoured methods of teaching have had to relinquish their exclusive rights.

[2] *Information scolaire*, 1956 (photo Robert Doisneau)

◄ [1] Nairobi, 1990 (photo Eddy Posthuma de Boer)      **THE CLASSROOM DETHRONED** 23

# The articulated classroom

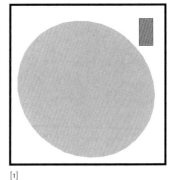

[1]

Wherever traditional classroom-based education is not given exclusively and so the teacher is not the constant focus of attention, the need exists for nooks and niches to work in, more or less screened-off or shielded places where one or more pupils can concentrate on their own work. This was mainly the case in schools with alternative pedagogy with their exclusive ideas about education, where children were encouraged to work independently. These schools had trouble working with rectangular, unarticulated classrooms. They often began life out of necessity in large former houses where they were happy to find the bays, nooks and corners they encountered there. This satisfied the need for more particularized spaces. These spaces not originally designed for teaching purposes often proved to provide the ideal spatial conditions for individual-oriented education and for pupils to find a place where they could work on their own. These places were more suited to uncustomary uses and you felt less under scrutiny by teachers than in an excessively surveyable unarticulated space. The more articulated or modelled a space is, the more possibilities for more differentiated learning it has to offer.

An unarticulated rectangular classroom lends itself best to instruction, the unidirectional transfer of knowledge that forms the basis of teacher-fronted lessons. This primitive paradigm gives teachers the ideal overview of their pupils. An articulated space by contrast is less easily surveyable and provides more places for different groups or individuals to engage in different activities simultaneously in a room without being unduly distracted by each other. So the number of options are greater here, there being several centres of attention rather than just the one.

A condition of learning in which children work on different subjects alone or in groups parallels the need for more workplaces of different sizes and spatial quality. This requires not just that the classroom be articulated but also encourages colonizing what was once the corridor and domesticating it as an 'outside area' of the learning territory. This form of decentralization compromises the hegemony of the classroom as an autonomous bastion, so that children leave it to collect what they need 'outside'. In time, this need to also work beyond the classrooms became greater. It increasingly

[1, 2] Articulation leads to multiple centres

[3, 5, 6] Classroom, Apollo schools, Amsterdam

[4, 7-10] Classroom, Montessori school, Delft

[3]

[4]

**Articulated classroom**

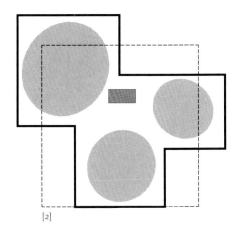

[2]

gave rise to a situation at primary schools comparable to that at secondary schools, where pupils move through the school, visiting a different subject room for each period.

So the classroom as the sole, permanent teaching space is a thing of the past. Slowly but surely the corridors are being enlisted so that the teaching-learning territory is coming to occupy the entire school. The primary school classroom has therefore evolved into a home base; a familiar environment to fall back on.

[7]

[5]

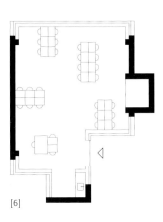

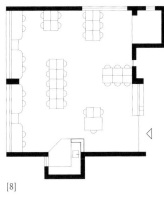

[6]

[8]

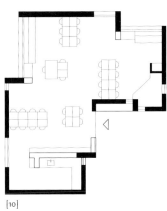

[10]

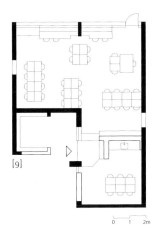

[9]

0  1    2m

# 1st Montessori School, Corellistraat, Amsterdam, 1927

A.R. Hulshoff

Amsterdam's Public Montessori schools were built from 1923 on, at the instigation of the city's Alderman for Education, Eduard Polak. Polak had more than 200 schools erected in this capacity. As he was an advocate of innovation in pedagogy, several of these were for the Montessori and Dalton systems. The only difference between the Montessori schools and the others, built with great care by Public Works, lay in the two extra spaces added to each classroom. Each of the classrooms was given a tiled 'kitchen space' where water could be splashed around and watering cans filled to water the many plants in the classroom – each child has at least one plant to look after. The large low-lying sink unit means that the children are free to go about painting and modelling in clay independently. In addition, every classroom was provided with a 'resting room', a side area much like a sitting room. This addition to the main classroom space is separated from it by a passage lined on both sides by fixed cupboards with glass doors. Fixed benches with cushions where you can read or lie down stand round about. This is where you can withdraw to from the bustle of the class so as to concentrate on your work. Every child, we should recall, has their own work to do. A sheet can be hung in the passage so that behind it plays and sketches can be prepared unseen by others. When these are enacted for the class, the sheet becomes the stage curtain. There are no fixed workplaces for pupils in this general-use side/ sitting room; it is extra space!

The classroom with annexes had a surface area of about 95 m², a size quite unattainable by today's skimping standards, though it was exceptional even in those days. These annexes made the classroom even more of an autonomous entity of several rooms, as if a dwelling-house. The completeness of the equipment in these class-

[1]

[2]

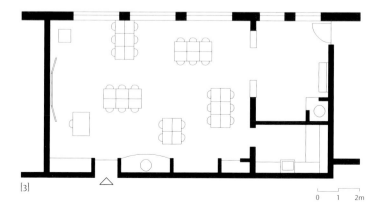

[3]

0   1   2m

rooms did nothing to advance contact with the rest of the school, at least physically. You were allowed a fleeting visit to other classes only in privileged situations, for instance when you 'did the rounds' to give tea to the other teachers or took round sweets or cakes on your birthday, or were chosen by a special friend to help them do this on theirs. Then it was the older classes, where everything was bigger, that impressed you the most.

Of all the schools you visit during your life, it's always the first one you attended that leaves the biggest impression on you, and for an architect it must have a considerable bearing on their practice later on.
In my own memory, Christmas was the only occasion that school life spilled out beyond the bastions of the classrooms. Then all the pupils performed and watched short plays in the gymnasium, the only space large enough for this purpose. This stage event was the high point of the year. Once all classes had entered in succession and taken their place, no-one was allowed to move.

So you did see each other, but it was hardly what you would call a social event.

A visit I paid in May 2005, more than 60 years on, revealed that little had changed in all that time and that everything still worked according to the original philosophy. In those days schools were built to last, with solid walls and sustainable materials. Not just that, the Montessori method of education, revolutionary though it had been in the beginning, has remained remarkably consistent in its ideas and their

[4]

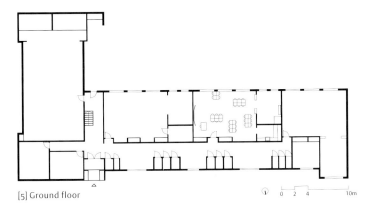

[5] Ground floor

application in day-to-day practice. Only the original round iron stoves, hidden behind attractive metal railings, had been replaced by secret workplaces. The corridors, cold and stony in my memory, were now being used by children at work.

But what was really eye-opening was seeing the dimensions of the teaching spaces again. The difference between 95 m² then and the 50 m² we get today illustrates in shocking terms how we, though immeasurably richer than we were in 1927, are saddled with a sorry pack of tightwads – a far cry from the idealism of the Amsterdam aldermen of those days.

[1]

[2]

[3]

[4]

## Montessori School, Valkeveen, 1926
Brinkman & Van der Vlugt

It can not be generally known that the architects of the Van Nelle factory and other pellucid 'functionalist' buildings had once designed a tiny Montessori School. This restrained and almost entirely inward-looking building of traditional construction, the very opposite of their later work, has just one classroom but this is so strongly modelled as to give the impression of being several unmediated rooms. Identical bay-window-like additions to the taller central space, separated from it by arches and extending symmetrically to four sides, suggest a Villa Rotonda in miniature. This space, being articulated, is scarcely suited to traditional teacher-fronted lessons but lends itself all the more to decentralized use as in the Montessori system where many different activities take place simultaneously. It comes as quite a surprise, then, to come across this exceptionally early example of an articulated teaching space.

[1]

[2]

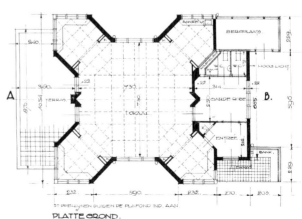

[3]

# Montessori School, Delft, 1960-1966

[4]

In the early 1960s the administrative board of the Delft Montessori School, mainly consisting of progressive-minded professor's wives, commissioned us to to design new premises. We gladly seized the opportunity to finally design a classroom form better tailored to Montessori ideas, in view of the little that had evolved in this field since the 1930s.

According to the Montessori method, children generally work individually on self-chosen activities. The necessary concentration differs with the type of work; not only that, the capacity for concentration in one pupil is not the same as that in another. One child doing their sums can be distracted by others who are, say, rehearsing a play or experimenting with magnets. This is often seen as a disadvantage of individual training, not entirely without justification.

The space should be organized in such a way as to prevent pupils from distracting each other unduly. As a theoretical model for the

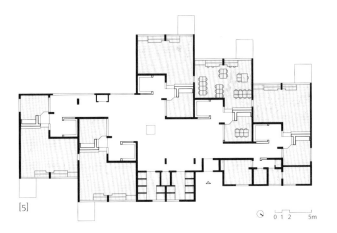

[5]

Montessori classroom, we chose the snail's shell with its increasing protection inwards and increasing openness outwards. Translate this spatially into a school and you get a sequence of zoning running from seclusion and privacy to successively more 'public' and social space. Classrooms, secluded but without an explicit barrier, spill over into the common zone of a central space. Ulti-mately, this configuration of an unbroken articulated space opening outwards from an enclosed core was rendered as an L-shaped classroom, articulated in zones from introverted to extroverted.
These zones are shielded from each other spatially so that those engaged in more intellectual work are least distracted by the more active painters and clay modellers. To this end, the floor of the less visually busy portion of the classroom is set several treads higher so that the 'creative' part is even less conspicuous from the 'intellectual' part.

[1]

[3]

0   1   2m

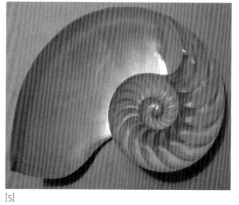

[4]

[2]

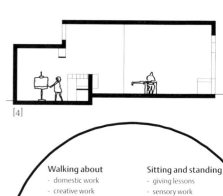

[5]

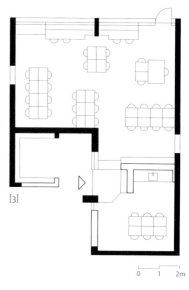

**Walking about**
- domestic work
- creative work
- projects

**Sitting and standing**
- giving lessons
- sensory work
- much help needed

**Hall**
- working outside classroom
- alone or together
- as a class or not

**At rest**
- concentration
- intellectual work
- less supervision needed

[6]

[7] ▶

# The classroom as home base

Classrooms of schools for secondary education have changed from group rooms to subject rooms. They used to be entirely the domain of the teachers while the pupils, without a place of their own, wandered through the school like nomads along a route dictated by the sequence of lessons.

In a traditional primary school, each group does have its own classroom but here the teacher calls the tune. The feeling of safety and homecoming depends on the nature and at times the mood of that teacher. Classrooms in fact belong to the teachers and the pupils are visitors. Although they know that is where they belong, it is debatable whether the pupils really feel at home there. For this, their own influence and responsibility should extend further than, say, a few pictures on the wall. They should be able to have a say in where they sit in the classroom and how that space is fitted out. And it goes without saying that this calls into question the presence in the classroom of a class teacher.

Whenever children spill out of the classroom to enlarge their field of attention, as is the new trend at primary schools, whether to seek out a place to work independently or take part in special lessons, there is the likelihood of disengagement. This is often the case in secondary school education but at least at that age it is compensated for to a degree by the pupils' keen interest in and attraction to each other. At the primary school, by contrast, pupils have a greater need for something permanent to fall back on, not exclusively a teacher but most of all a readily identifiable and familiar environment. This place should be something of a 'nest' from which you take off and to which you keep returning; a place to leave your things, to fall back on and to meet up again. A floor plan where everything spills into everything else, like a spatial continuum, with no thresholds and therefore no territorial divisions, may well be the ultimate consequence of a school where children find their own way around, armed with a personal laptop and mobile phones. And yet a "'safe nest' – familiar surroundings where you know that your things are safe and where you can concentrate without being disturbed by others – is something each individual needs as much as each group. Without this there can be no collaboration with others. If you don't have a place that you can call your own you don't know where you stand! There can be no adventure without a home-base to return to: everyone needs some kind of nest to fall back on."[1] Could this established principle of biological origin simply be switched off? And that brings us straight to the avian duality of nest and flight.[2] Birds fly through space with a clear view of their food and return to the nest, the place that gives them protection.

So schools must provide 'nests', places with sufficient shelter, tending towards a centre and with dimensions that permit individuals but also groups of varying size to immerse themselves in their work. And then there is the surrounding space which arouses your curiosity and incites confrontation. Yet even in the physical safety of the nest you can enter the most exciting and dangerous virtual worlds, engrossed in a book or computer screen.

As a basic facility, the classroom is an age-old example of space for learning, in the sense of instruction. It provides the safety and security children generally feel they need when away from home and in a group situation not of their choosing.

The 'class' can take you under its wing, you can face the teacher from a common position, support one another and together present a social front as the group to which you belong. And where classrooms are becoming increasingly open as in modern schools, relinquishing their autonomy in the process, pupils tend to mingle more during work hours with those from other classes. The situation is getting more complex and it's up to the architect to spatially support these new potentials and keep it all clearly organized so that children have enough to go on in order to find their way about.

There is much to be said for having doors to link adjoining classrooms. By connecting intervening partitions to the outer wall with a glazed section with a door in it, classrooms can be linked when necessary without forfeiting their autonomy. Incredibly, not a few teachers are dead set against this strategy. At one time it was in the regulations that teachers were to keep an eye on classrooms adjoining their own whenever a class was briefly left to its own devices. It is also a way to conduct joint projects: you can enter the neighbouring classroom directly, much like adjacent gardens with a gap in the fence. It also helps you to become more aware of the presence of others and increases the view out from the classroom, visually but also psychologically; it enlarges your perspective. The evolution of the traditional classroom as a bastion for instruction to the classroom as home base, from where the children spill out more and more frequently and which they can always fall back on, is the result of a successive increase in the number of individual activities among more and more groups and individuals. Where once it was only groups of 30 to 45 pupils who concentrated collectively on a single point, now the group focuses increasingly on different centres of attention. Spatially, this gives an ever greater need for places, spatial entities, not sealed off but open and inviting, places where you still can concentrate and feel at home.

We can distinguish successive stages of spatial development:

1 an increase in the number of places by differentiating the rectangular classroom with nooks, ancillary spaces, bays etc;

2 the addition of a zone between classroom and corridor (the threshold) which can be used as and when necessary to enlarge the learning area;

3 the change in the classroom's duty from place of instruction to home base. The group is more often incomplete or absent as more and more learning activities are being held elsewhere in the school;

4 the emergence of a learning landscape where classrooms shrink or disappear altogether.


With classrooms disappearing entirely to be taken up in an open learning landscape, the need for a home base is felt all the more, for a place for the children to fall back on, a place they feel responsible for and where they can leave their belongings. It is not enough to have lockers in anonymous surroundings so that pupils wander daily through the building like nomads. There has to be a space where they can engage socially with others of their group or year.

Not everyone is equipped to stand alone in a world rife with opportunities, challenges and surprises without having a recognizable and familiar smaller unit where they have a sense of belonging. To satisfy this spatial condition is a new challenge for architects, one that may give entirely different shape to the idea of a home base if the classroom were indeed to disappear completely.

1 *Lessons for Students in Architecture*, p. 28
2 See *Lessons for Students in Architecture*, p. 28 and *Lessons 2*, p. 25

Class display case, De Eilanden Montessori primary school, Amsterdam

## Montessori School, Delft, 1960-1966

"The classrooms of the Delft Montessori School can be regarded as autonomous units, little homes in themselves, all situated along the school hall, as a communal street. The teacher or 'mother' of each home decides together with the children what the place will look like, and therefore what kind of atmosphere it will have. Each classroom has its own small cloakroom, instead of the usual shared excessive number of pegs on almost every wall so that they can't be used for anything else. And if each classroom were to have its own toilet this too would contribute to improving the children's sense of responsibility. You can imagine the children in each class keeping their own 'home' clean, as birds do with their nest. At that time, though, the educational authorities turned down this proposal on the grounds that boys and girls should have separate toilets – as if they have them at home! – which would mean twice as many.

"Montessori education does include so-called housekeeping duties as part of the daily programme. So much emphasis is placed on having the children look after their environment, thereby strengthening their emotional affinity with it. Each child, too, has their own plant which they have to look after.

"A further step towards a more personal approach to the children's daily surroundings would be to make it possible to regulate heating per classroom. This would heighten the children's awareness of the phenomenon of warmth as well as making them more energy-conscious. Now, forty years on, these aspects are relevant as never before and there is all the more reason to take them into account when designing a school.

"The domain of a particular group should be respected as much as possible by 'outsiders'. That is why there are certain risks attached

to so-called multifunctional use. If a schoolroom is used for local activities in the evening, everything gets shifted and perhaps not returned to its original place. Clay models of animals left out to dry can be accidentally damaged, or the smallest weight from the classroom scales goes missing.

"It is important for children to be able to display the things they have made in, say, the handwork lesson without fear of them being damaged, and to leave out whatever still needs finishing without it being moved or 'tidied away' by 'strangers'. Even a thorough sprucing-up by the cleaning lady is enough to leave you feeling quite lost in your own space the next morning.

"A schoolroom, conceived as the domain of a group, can show its own identity to the rest of the school by displaying the projects and other work done by this group. This can be done informally by using the partition between hall and classroom for pinning things on and making windows with generous cills in the partition.

"A small display case, preferably with its own lighting, is a challenge to the group to present its offerings in a more formal way. Classroom exteriors can then function as 'shop windows' for the group to display its 'wares'."3

In this way each class can present a signature that others can relate to, and which marks the transition between a classroom and the communal area.

When designing a school you can create the conditions for a greater sense of responsibility and thus a greater feeling for tending and fitting out a space, which in turn creates a greater feeling for tending and fitting out an area in general. This is how users become inhabitants.

3 Adapted from *Lessons for Students in Architecture*, pp. 28-30

► [1] Entrance to classroom, Montessori school, Delft

# From corridor to learning street

As the emphasis in modern education on classroom-based methods dropped steadily and more individual education and group-based work rose, the traditional classroom came to be considered 'too small'. Before this need became general, many schools of alternative pedagogy had already gained experience in this field but invariably it meant a greater surface area. In the fullness of time the need grew not just for more square metres but most of all for more places for the greatest number of children to be able to concentrate, undisturbed by others.

Because this development ran parallel to what was a systematic reduction of the surface area due to cutbacks in expenditure on education, it was a logical next step to look at ways of making the corridor area double as a work zone.

Add to that the influx then still getting under way of immigrants whose varying backgrounds and especially the language barrier gave cause to radically revise the way education was traditionally organized. Another cause of differences in standards in class was the trend of closing down specialized schools for children with behavioral and learning difficulties so that these ended up at regular schools. So on top of the division into years there was now a division into standards requiring the provision of much smaller places for teaching and learning.

As a result, the partition walls between classrooms and corridors became more open, raising the claim made by each class on a portion of corridor, which gradually came to be regarded as part of their domain. In time, the centre of classroom teaching and learning activity shifted to the entrails of the building.

So classrooms no longer acted as bastions with just windows to the outside world and turning away from the corridors, but instead opened up to them and even encroached

[2]  Space for the smallest children, giving onto rooftop play terrace. De Vogels primary school, Oegstgeest

◄  [1]  Built-in worktop along window, Montessori school, Delft on them. This changed the nature of these cavernous, chilly ancillary spaces, which were usually too long and too tall and often dimly lit, into living and working space theoretically equal in quality to the classrooms themselves and deserving of daylight and sun. How long ago was it that children who didn't pay attention were sent out of the classroom into the corridor, banished into empty space, beyond the territory of the group? There you were at the mercy of the cold, the loneliness and most of all the boredom that led you to take a look in the pockets of all those hundreds of coats just hanging there. And then there was the humiliation when someone walked past.

If corridors are to be made 'inhabitable' as true extensions of the classrooms, they will require a complete change in both look and lighting. All coats and the other attributes that invariably turn corridors into endless cloakrooms would have to be moved from the walls and out of sight and replaced by tables and equipment that evoke a working atmosphere and focus the attention. Only then will associations with the old paradigm vanish and the necessary wall space be freed for the workplaces that brought this all on. The main thing is to make the greatest imaginable number of workplaces and make them as differentiated as possible. That will give you a building equipped throughout for education, that is, in the wider sense of learning.

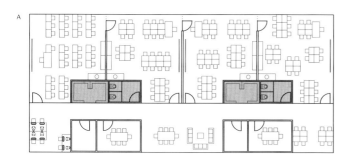

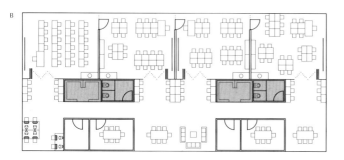

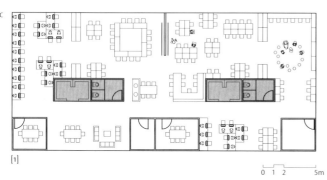

[1]

[2]

[3]

0  1  2        5m

A  Regular classrooms
B  Classrooms with fold-away
   partitions between them and
   additional workplaces for
   collective use
C  Free plan

A, B and C have the same surface
area and contain the same number
of pupils

[2] Working outside the classroom, Apollo schools, Amsterdam

[3] Working outside the classroom, Montessori school, Delft

[4] Workplaces outside the classroom, De Salamander, Arnhem

[5, 6] Workplaces outside the
classroom, De Spil, Arnhem

It begins with workplaces outside the classroom where children can work individually or in groups, curriculum permitting. The more this proves to work better, the greater the claim every classroom will make on space beyond it. To consistently give up the corridor's role as an ancillary space is to embrace another paradigm which, although gaining ever more ground in the world of education, still clashes utterly with sociopolitical standards, suffocated as these are by the Dutch or otherwise European mania for regulating everything. There is also the persistent fear that serious education will suffer from the greater freedom and responsibility with which the children are entrusted, that it will cause them to fail examinations, depriving them of the certificate they need to score well in the employment stakes. The increasing focus in society on results means that 'safe' traditional patterns in education persist. One of these is that lessons are given inside classrooms rather than outside them.

In their barest, most stripped-down form, corridors serve as circulation space for accessing and connecting the rooms on either side of them. This is the notion we encounter in old traditional school buildings but also in hospitals and office buildings, indeed wherever the network of corridors is merely dimensioned to suit the expected flow of people. So the corridor is regarded as 'clearance' or intervening space: admit-

[4]

[5]

[6]

[1]

[2]

[3]

[4]

[1]  Learning square beyond the
classroom, Titaan, Hoorn

[2]  Harmonica partitions to
classroom, Titaan, Hoorn

[3, 4]  Corridors, J. van Biesen,
school, Arnhem, 1932

tedly necessary but unproductive and so of no use. Of course, it can be used to get rid of some of the energy of overactive youngsters by letting them run it off there.

At one time, the corridors and stairwells in schools were made relatively large to accommodate cloakrooms and take up the expected crush at such places. There was also the spectre of a mass of overactive children who have had to remain still for too long and whose frustrated energy, on being released, would explode in an inexorable surge of pulling and shoving, all at a time when classes were emptying simultaneously. Staircases could never be wide enough, for this reason. All the same, they would remain the major bottleneck where all corridors converged, where the sound seemed to pile up in the reverberating stone or brick cavity and where pushing could lead to accidents. And yet it was the stern and imposing entrance and grand staircase that gave the building its serious air and status. And, only the central staircase made you realize that the upper and lowers floors, which were barely connected spatially, were meant to act as an entity. Yet their separation gave the upper storey a greater status: this was where the older classes were, where you had to work hard.

In the Netherlands, school-building is subsidized by the government and consequently forever bound by strict standards in programme and surface area, not least to divide up the budgets fairly. During the past twenty years, it has been systematically subjected to cuts in expenditure.[4] This has focused attention unduly on the number and size of classrooms to the extent that these quantities have become virtually inviolable. Inadvertently, quantity scores higher than quality in the building programmes, as these are more a product of bureaucracy than of pedagogical instruction. This is a difficult construct to dismantle. Add to this an accepted percentage of overhead costs (for wall partitions, maintenance and plant and all other necessary if scarcely tolerated aspects) in square metres, though this surface area is constantly being gnawed at in a move to keep costs down. In the government's perspective, a good architect is one who is able to organize their plan as rationally as possible; the 'ideal architect' makes the seemingly inviolable 'teaching space' as big as possible and keeps the rest, including the corridors, to a minimum. The more conservative teachers, who feel safest within the walls of their own classroom, are all too keen to go along with this. The paradox is that it is only by breaking through this institutionalized economy-driven system of standards that a more efficient use of space, one more responsive to today's challenges, can be achieved.

Nor is it just a more efficient use of what space is available (or made available) that takes us to the concept of a school without bare circulation corridors where every corner is a potential corner of learning; such a differentiated place capacity is equally desirable from a pedagogical point of view. An explosive increase in the number of different-aptitude groups, particularly due to the lack of Dutch language skills among immigrants but also to the rising use of computers at school, continues to fuel the need for places for discrete learning situations. Increasingly, pupils are working individually or in small groups. Another factor is the ever dwindling supply of teachers, so that the idea of pupils working independently is a logical possible solution, be it more for pragmatic than for didactic motives.

Meanwhile architects should concern themselves less with pedagogical aspects and more with the spatial conditions that could be supportive of these. It is in just this area that architecture is the ideal means of providing fundamental steps towards a spatial order with the school building's accessible spaces articulated in such a way that the place capacity is raised to the maximum.

Outside the classroom you come into contact with others engaged in school activities you yourself are not perhaps ready for yet, which is precisely why they have a magical, galvanizing effect on you. You acquire insight into what there is on offer. This way, you get a taste of what you are going to be confronted with later.

This broader perspective on teaching and learning is not to be found in a building brief, this being set quantitatively. The extent to which this image does in fact materialize depends largely on the spatial conditions the architect is able to bring to bear in his design.

It's all about finding the right balance between places with the greatest diversity in dimensions and such qualities as lighting and 'cover'. The physical cohesion between them should present an overview of it all, so that everything has its own recognizable place within the dynamic of a whole that is constantly changing. Over and again, places are appropriated by others and appropriated differently. In more precise terms, these have to be potential places where an individual or group can settle temporarily.

We must always design in such a way that both components and totality are always open to be appropriated and so incite activity. And if that holds true anywhere, it is in schools.

If architecture holds serious significance anywhere by providing the conditions that invite a richer world of experience, it is here where the riches of the learning environment are so dependent on the space they occupy.

At the end of the day, education, besides being about reading, writing and arithmetic, is about exploring the world. It is not just obtaining insight that is important but, increasingly, accumulating interest and love for the riches our world has to offer. This happens in interactive situations that could be stimulated more by the physical environment than designers are prepared to concede.

4 Education the Dutch way: all school types measured against the
   same financial yardstick; educational cock-and-bull stories
   launched as a pretext for cutbacks in expenditure; classroom surface area continually being reduced (student-teacher ratio); State-
   allotted Council subsidies based on the number of pupils and
   classes; risk run by councillors through demographic uncertainty; managers instead of inspectors…

# Threshold space between classroom and corridor

The claim on space outside your territory automatically changes the nature of what it is that separates classrooms from corridors. With corridors changing from circulation area to work area comes an ever greater need for openness; there needs to be visual contact from the classes with those working outside, so that these remain under the watchful eye of the teacher and retain a sense of belonging despite their physical detachment. In time, though, they will come to move independently throughout the entire building as the classroom continues to relinquish its status as sole study area.

This working outside the classroom, though close by, brings with it the need for a transitional area that belongs to both corridor and classroom and can be interpreted in terms of its context.

In principle this is a threshold area: it "provides the key to the transition and connection between areas with divergent territorial claims and, as a place in its own right, it constitutes, essentially, the spatial condition for the meeting and dialogue between areas of different orders."[5]

In the bureaucratic culture of accountancy they cling to in the Netherlands mainly in an attempt on the part of teachers not to lose ground, the surface area of the classroom is sacrosanct. You can read from it not merely the history of the authorities' attitude to teaching and learning over the years; the dimensions of the classrooms have attained the status of a right to be defended by the schools at any price. If we go on to consider that the corridors alongside them are regarded exclusively as circulation space and their dimensions consequently kept to a minimum, it becomes clear that there is no place for a zone between classroom and corridor area, at least in accounting terms. It would require considerable persuasive powers to organize such a zone. After all, if you consider this threshold area to be part of the classroom – and there is in fact no other option – the classroom surface area remaining for teacher-fronted lessons would be correspondingly smaller, which is not likely to appeal to teachers.

When the threshold zone is shaped correctly and with the appropriate spatial means, it can give a smooth transition between corridor area and classroom that is more an articulation than a closure. This will leave the whole larger instead of smaller, even though this zone is arguably at the cost of the classroom surface area. With the classroom opened up and the pupils spilling out, the space for education, or rather the learning space as a whole, has become bigger.

5 *Lessons for Students in Architecture*, p. 32

# Apollo Schools, Amsterdam, 1980-1983

"If the space between classrooms has been used to create porchlike areas, as in the Amsterdam Montessori school, these areas can serve as proper workplaces where you can study on your own, i.e. not in the classroom but not shut out either. These places consist of a work-surface with its own lighting and a bench enclosed by a low wall. In order to regulate the contact between classroom and hall as subtly as possible half-doors have been installed here, whose ambiguity can generate the right degree of openness towards the hall while offering the required seclusion from it, both at the same time, in each situation."[6]

As a pupil, you feel the trust you were given to work beyond the immediate supervision of the teacher. As a teacher, you are not entirely screened off from what happens 'out there'. Since computers were introduced at primary schools these places are regularly used as computer work stations. Here as in Delft there is a display case next to the door, a tiny museum and shop window for each class.

6 *Lessons for Students in Architecture*, p. 31

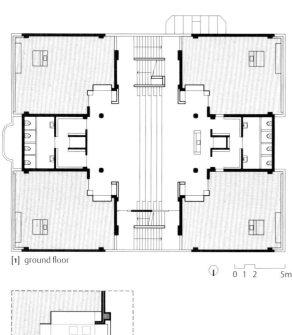

[1] ground floor

0 1 2    5m

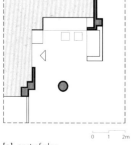

[2] part of plan

0   1    2m

[3]

# De Vogels Primary School, Oegstgeest, 1998-2000

The transitional area between classroom and corridor, here shaped between the cloakroom and the toilet units, is opened to the classroom through a regular door as well as a sliding door. It invites tables to be placed against the side walls of the adjoining cloakroom and toilet units and against the rear wall of the wet services block in the middle of the space, as workplaces belonging to the classroom but located in the corridor. So it is important to have roof lights above this particular zone as good lighting, especially daylight, lends quality and centrality to a place as a magnet for activity.

The spatial conditions of the in-between zone, created with marginal dimensions, not only hold out the opportunity to work outside the classroom but actually stimulate such activity. The corridor area is part of the classrooms in places and thus is more than just circulation space.

[1]

[2]

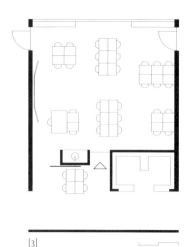

[3]

0  1  2m

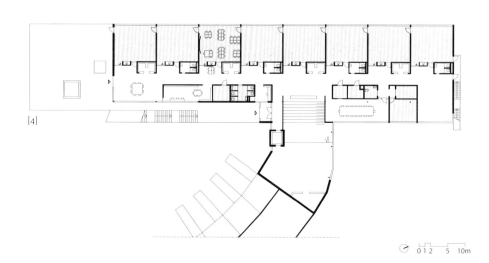

[4]

0 1 2  5  10m

## De Eilanden Montessori Primary School, Amsterdam, 1996-2002

Although this school in fact has only 'regular' classrooms, these always function in open mode. Pupil activity takes place all over. There is almost no difference between the classrooms and what you might call the corridor area.

This comes close to a situation in which the distinction between corridors and rooms is entirely erased. This is certainly due to the pedagogical ideas of this Montessori school and it is difficult to assess what contribution the spatial arrangement makes to it. But, when you see that pupils are at work in every corner and that the space is articulated so as to soften almost all divisions between places, it then seems clear that the work ambience felt everywhere is largely due to the designed spatial conditions. Articulating the space so as to create a multitude of places contributes to an ambience in which as many children as possible, alone or in groups, can work without disturbing each other, though they continually feel each other's presence.

[5]

[6]

[7]

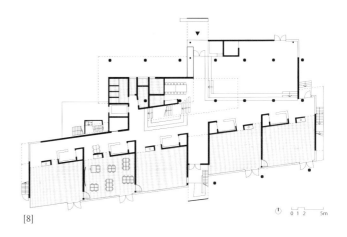

[8]

0 1 2    5m

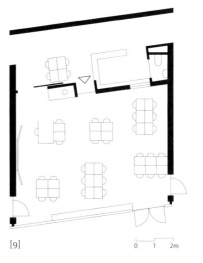

[9]

0    1    2m

# Extended Schools, Arnhem, 2004-2007

For the five schools in Arnhem, assembled in three so-called Extended Schools, we deliberately chose a configuration whereby the classrooms are no longer closed-off bastions but can be opened up fully to the corridor areas using glass accordion partitions. These corridor areas are nothing like the circulation zones so regularly resorted to; they are shared prefatory spaces fully fitted out as additional work areas. Here the fear teachers harbour about losing ground is quite unfounded. The ongoing discourse on education has unquestionably brought a greater openness towards new possibilities. So an open learning area was accepted without compromise. Even so, having the largest possible sliding or folding walls is not enough in itself. It does allow much coming and going but there can only be workplaces if you make corners for them. Besides this openness of classrooms, it is about creating as closely as possible to the classrooms the greatest number of low-profile spots where tables can be placed and places made, so that the work area is continuous.

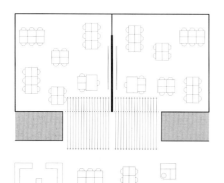
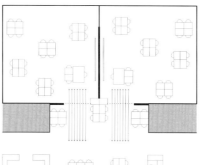

[1]

[2]

[3]

# Learning landscape

How should architects respond to the countless initial steps being taken here, there and everywhere to change or renew education? Until now, the classroom has been an implacable spatial entity erected round the unambiguous relationship between teacher and pupil and an unequivocal pedagogical paradigm. Once it is abandoned to make way for other forms of learning, it is up to architects to find new, more stimulating spatial conditions and forms.

The ultimate environment for changes in learning where pupils are expected to be more independent, is an entirely open floor plan which can be divided up freely with lightweight partitions that can be moved around to suit every new occasion and change in needs. Teachers should then be willing and able to make those organizational changes themselves. Indeed, up to a point they are better equipped to do this than the architect, especially when it comes to their own programmatic requirements, though it does require an understanding of spatial order to make the most efficient and practical use of the available surface area. So a joint effort should do the trick.

The notion of the classroom-less school has reappeared. This school type had been fairly popular in the USA in the 1950s and '60s but failed to establish itself.
In the meantime, the 'learning landscape' with the office landscape as forerunner (at least in the Netherlands) looks like it's here to stay as a spatial form for schools, though the spatial repercussions are considerable. The teachers are expected to suffer most, whether the architect intervenes or not, as it will be hard not having a classroom, their traditional bastion, to fall back on.

A learning landscape bears some resemblance to a Montessori classroom but is very much bigger. In it, pupils in different age groups work individually on a variety of subjects under the supervision of several teachers. Criticism, justified or otherwise, persistently levelled at this method of working invariably concludes that 'not all children are suited to this type of education'. It is a mild form of criticism of unorthodox education, which is said to make excessive demands on pupils and teachers alike.
What architects can learn from all this is that they should not be beguiled into deploying a minimalism of entirely free plans; these can be fitted out 'flexibly', it is true, but completely lack the permanence and protection pupils can withdraw to if they are to be able to concentrate. There is a reciprocity of educational objectives on one hand and physical possibilities on the other, where what is desired, whether or not driven by social challenges, is simply not possible at present, certainly when you consider the tight budgets that lead to a lack of space instead of the extra surface area essential to every context involving change. A paradoxical situation then.

The shadow of the walls between classrooms will persist to begin with. For the moment, the emphasis will be on the possibilities of combining classrooms, preferably with handy sliding and accordion partitions. Teachers expect miracles of these, but practice has proved that these partitions are scarcely used and merely get in the way. As traditional orthodox forms of education fall away, new spatial conditions will come into play, being basically a multitude of workplaces for smaller groups simultaneously occupied with as many activities.

Not that this necessarily excludes classroom-type spaces. There will always be a call for rooms for instruction. Partitions that model the space at room scale will not rule out a free plan providing they are open to the side where the corridor used to be. An entirely unarticulated space which teachers theoretically can fit out and divide up at their discretion, say with cupboards and other movables, tends to degenerate into an illegible mess. The greater the emphasis on the component parts, the less visible the overall picture and the greater the danger that the parts will come to obscure the whole from view entirely and consequently get lost.

The big picture has to be clear and well-organized, and give a broad impression of what is on offer and the challenges involved. This requires built spatial unity and cohesion, a collective structure, and for that alone you need an architect.

The learning landscape is continually in a state of flux because of the succession of teachers, subjects, resources and ideas. Its major quality is being able to absorb and adapt to these changes, at the same time patently showing up the disadvantages of the rigid system of classrooms.

The idea of a landscape makes its entrance wherever individual freedom is suggested and structure is felt to be unduly imposed from above. Situations and processes that seem to evolve unaided, as if naturally, tend to appeal more and appear more democratic than those that are orchestrated and controlled.

In a landscape setting, then, emphasis seems to be on individual expression. Everyone needs a degree of control over their

immediate surroundings and needs to know where they stand there. This does however jeopardize the common interest which is regarded with distrust, although the communal with its wealth of individual acts of expression needs keeping in balance and so should certainly not be neglected. A landscape is a structure too, of course, kept up by an often subtle balance of forces. Because this structure seems less coercive and is often invisible, when used to organize a school it clashes with the strong-arm tactics wielded by the classroom walls. The preference is to mark off compartments with freestanding components, cupboards for instance, to preserve an element of uncertainty. Flexibility is the spatial equivalent of freedom; the freedom not to have to fix anything remains an irresistible illusion and gives the impression of having conquered time. Spatial cohesion is an absolute must.

Complete freedom, then, is a myth that mostly prevails in the minds of those who are not free. Freedom ultimately takes account of nothing and no-one; freedom is boundless, like a river bursting its banks, unbridled, unrestrained and all-engulfing. Space must be a bedding that gives direction to all individual forces, bundling them as it were into a common flow.

It is the architect who each time has to guarantee the collective order and express it spatially as the most permanent possible framework in which to house the more specific but also the more changeable of interests; a place where everything has its niche and everyone can feel comfortable, even when the situation, unpredictable as this is, can alter at any time. The correct structural theme, rather than limiting freedom, incites it instead.

Spatial articulation is all about finding an unchanging framework that can adapt to different situations without having to change itself. In that sense it is polyvalent and as a spatial ordering principle, able to adapt to ever new situations.

[1] Typical plan of primary school with classrooms and patio zones alongside free-form zones with a variety of places

[2]
A Help desk / teaching staff base
B Mini-theatre
C Living room / home base

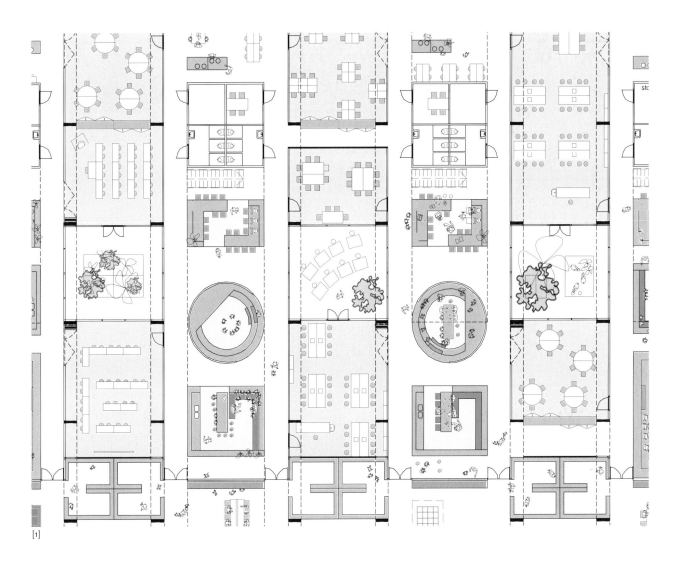

[1]

A

B

C

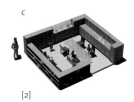

[2]

# Open Schools, USA

In the 1950s there were already experiments being done in the United States with schools without classrooms, where numbers of groups were brought together in vast indoor spaces, not that this ever produced anything like a distinct building type. Omitting the partitions between classrooms may impact on the social pattern but is not enough to create its own space. So spatially it failed to satisfy what was needed to give groups working alongside each other the privacy they require. In other words, spacious does not mean space. Photos of the 'open school' reveal an assertive position on teaching and learning, yet surely the different groups, occupying a collective field of vision without the slightest spatial modelling, must have caused each other considerable inconvenience.

We see here a striking similarity with the almost simultaneous rise of open plan offices, the office landscape. Here, too, many had difficulty concentrating and were continually inconvenienced by one another. Countermanding this is the greater sense of community and the galvanizing effect a view of each other and each other's work can have.

These partitionless, spacious expanses mean freedom before anything else; freedom from too many elements that are fixed and fixing, and the opening-up of possibilities for a new agenda.

What it really boils down to in education – and here we must abandon the comparison with the office landscape – is giving and receiving guidance. The onerous task for teachers of keeping everyone quiet and occupied is not enough in the long run. We only make real progress when the work environment itself manages to bring about a good working atmosphere, without additionally burdening the teachers, so that these can give guidance to their pupils during lessons all the more intensively.

[1]

[2]

[1, 2] Granada Community School, California, USA

## Hellerup Skole, Gentofte, Copenhagen, DK, 2002
## Arkitema

From outside, this internally remarkable building looks much like a regular industrial shed, revealing nothing of the true nature of its extraordinary contents. Even its entrance is relatively inconspicuous. It is only after entering it through an enlarged gateway where all the children leave their shoes, that the unusual set-up is made clear. The Hellerup Skole is entirely open save for some dedicated subject rooms. Half-height walls of lockers are all that separate the learning zones or 'home areas' from the main space, dominated by wide stairs doubling as seats, that draws the three storeys together. In the home areas are enclosed hexagonal pavilion-like structures equipped with seating, around which group lessons can be given to 15 to 20 children. There are also places shaped by cupboards, benches and small platforms two steps high. If there is a learning landscape anywhere it is here, where a scarcely discernible division into home areas for 75 to 100 pupils takes the place of classrooms. The school can accept 550 pupils all told, with a good 9 m² per pupil. This is something like three times as much as the standard stipulated for Dutch schools. It is probably an exception in Denmark too, although it is patently obvious that that country holds education in the highest esteem. This loose-fit approach to space does show what the possibilities are when there is no need to haggle over every square metre of ground. There is clearly a relaxed atmosphere because of this, making the learning space something of a workshop whose openness incites a degree of dedication.

You see children occupied with all kinds of 'creative' subjects; there are enough teachers in Denmark for this work and no lack of equipment either. There is even a corner where you can catch your breath and perhaps read in peace for once.

[4] Ground floor

0 2 4   10m

[3]

[6] Section

[5] First floor

[7] Second floor

This school unquestionably comes close to what we envisage as a space suited to teaching and learning today. It could be more clearly organized, though. You may be able to see and experience the periphery wherever you are, thanks in particular to the toplit central well reaching up all three storeys, but a more structured space would provide the order and clarity that would give everything a more permanent place. As it stands, it might come across as an excessively large and complex world with no clear orientation points and a prevailing uniformity in which children could get lost.

What is certain, though, is that the Hellerup Skole is a three-dimensional rendition of a new life-feeling that is much talked about but all too rare in reality. That in itself gives this school a significance that cannot be overestimated.

[1]

[2]

[3]

# Extension to De Jordaan 14th Montessori School, Amsterdam, 2004-2006

Existing buildings can also be adapted to suit education today, retaining the original main structure of classrooms on two sides of a corridor.

Here, what were at first isolated classrooms were assembled into one big space by making large openings in the walls of the old solid school building and inserting glass accordion partitions that can be folded away. The remaining wall piers become screens between departments. This gave rise to a single articulated space in which multiple groups of children can work together independently of one another but still with a feeling of community. So while retaining the building's structure, this gives a cohesive learning area with no sign of a corridor or of traditional classrooms. The different parts can be shut off to function as individual classrooms should the need arise. The term 'learning landscape' immediately brings to mind a large undivided area of floor. This does give the greatest freedom, in theory at least, but it is the articulation, here created by the remaining walls, that holds out the greatest potentials for use.

[4]

[5]

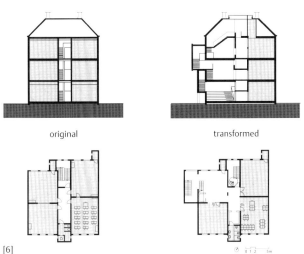

original                     transformed

[6]

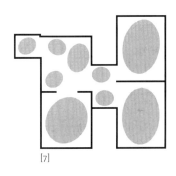

[7]

# De Monchy School, Arnhem, 2004-2007

In this school, part of De Spil Extended School in the Malburgen-West area of Arnhem, the classroom principle has been abandoned entirely. There are, however, glass accordion partitions that can be used to create classroom-like spaces should these be required.

The whole proceeds from a structural system that permits free floor spans of some 12 metres and therefore avoids such structural obstacles as supporting walls that could influence any potential subdivision of the space. The only fixed elements are the toilet blocks, cloakroom units and storage

units around which the space can be freely fitted out.

The school consists of 'zones' of 75 pupils with three teachers who can move from place to place or be consulted at a central help desk. If a learning landscape leads one to expect an entirely open space with

[1]

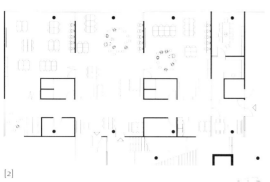

[2]

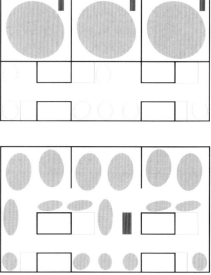

[3] Potential working-places

theoretically the greatest freedom, here the space is articulated by the fixed toilet blocks, storage units, cloakroom recesses and areas of partition wall resembling the remains of former classrooms. This opens up opportunities for place-making. All 'obstacles' are sited so as to encourage the greatest number of places suited to smaller or larger groups of pupils, in such a way that the circulation space between them is not hampered. Ultimately, the learning landscape thus articulated will offer more opportunities for individual workplaces than the seemingly greater freedom of an entirely open space. Besides, it is more difficult in the last-named instance to fall back at any time on a classroom-like subdivision.

[4]

[5]

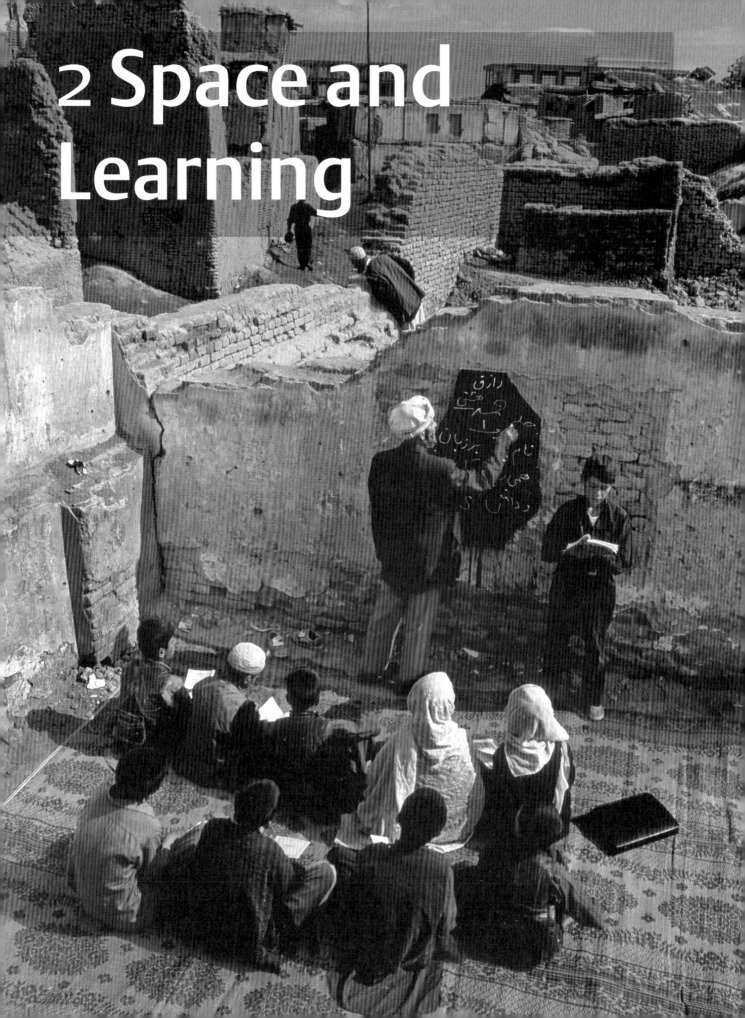

# 2 Space and Learning

# Space and learning

A sense of space comes from breaking down frameworks; from going further, deeper, higher, beyond the imaginable, the manageable, the known, the familiar. Like the acquisition of knowledge, a sense of space is a universal dimension in our minds. The surprising alliance of space with learning is something we cannot resist.

Indeed, many words and expressions relating to learning have spatial connotations. Develop, unearth, unfold, unveil, discover, explore, depth of meaning, aim too high, over one's head, sunk in thought, grasp of the material, get one's head round a fact, immerse oneself, disclose, unpack, insight, in-depth, dissect, open mind, search, fathom, bring home, fall into place...

We shouldn't see the brain as something that gets bigger and fuller when more and more information gets crammed in, drummed in or stored. The very term 'store', these days often linked to the digital world, is misleading as it suggests that our memories can become 'full' like that of a computer. If learning is the creating of paths in the brain, we should regard the brain as a network of links rather than a mass. Learning, absorbing new insights, enlarges and adds to this network so that less 'mass' remains and more space emerges. So if learning is removing barriers, blockages and restrictions, it is most of all opening up what was closed and thus creating space where there used to be mass.

Whatever the essence of learning may be, these links taking shape in the brain are paths that one might regard as three-dimensional, much like streets in a town, broad or narrow and branching out into alleyways where (according to an illustration by Freud) the most distant memories are housed. And as we learn more and the input increases, our brains don't get fuller but in fact gain space, a view of oneself, insights, prospects. This increased space in the brain can be looked upon as an increase in the number of associations, thereby forging new links between centres. To learn is to create order and coherence in the mind, to form structures where there had been none. Making space is applying structure where emptiness or chaos once prevailed. Learning, then, is a way of creating space in one's head; space for other aspects, ideas, relations, interpretations, associations. So learning is perhaps the finest imaginable approach to the concept of space.

# Schooling and learning

The designer of schools must inevitably engage with the dialectics of modern education. We are still building schools for education, where pupils are taught what society expects of them and what they have to know and be able to do to stand firm and develop in the society in which they are rooted. It is also about granting space for learning in a broader sense; it's not just a question of satisfying and thus adapting to the requirements made of you but of passing comment, not just accepting but thinking for yourself. Not just adapting to the world, then, but getting the world to adapt to you, to become suited to you.

Progressive educationalists see learning in its widest sense as a job for the school. But regrettably school buildings with their minimal spatial programmes are not designed for this purpose. Hence the often excessively ambitious pedagogic dreams are referred back to penny-pinching reality. Tight budgets mean rooms of minimum size with no leeway whatsoever for realizing something that extends further than the traditional study programme. (Indeed, the temporal as well the spatial programme of teachers and pupils is almost fully taken up by the inculcation and mastery of knowledge required to carry out the official school tests.) Ultimately, it is these official requirements that prevent broadening of the learning programme for teachers and pupils alike. As long as learning goes no further than conveying the officially accepted basic knowledge, all you need is a fixed spatial programme that follows the curriculum as painstakingly as possible: a row of classrooms with a corridor alongside.

But we don't get away with it that easily these days. Today's architect is entrusted with giving spatial form to the new ideas on education. This is a complex task, since a great deal has happened in recent years, such as:
• the arrival of the computer era. You still see many schools reluctantly setting aside

[1] A challenge for an inspired teacher: art expert and former museum director Rudi Fuchs set himself the task of firing young people's enthusiasm for classical painting, an area utterly unfamiliar to them (photo Bas Czerwinski)

[2, 3] Montessori College Oost, Amsterdam

[1]

[2]                                                                          [3]

corners or rooms for this purpose. Computers are changing not only education as a whole but also the spatial conditions that go with it;

- the emergence of greater differences between pupils in terms of background. Traditional classes are breaking down into smaller groups because of the differences in intellectual performance. This loss of homogeneity among the school population brings major social complications that pose new social challenges for the school;

- the arrival of pupils with diminished motivation and concentration, in all likelihood due to the deluge of stimuli in our modern world that causes distraction on all sides. How is a school to compete with television and the internet, with all the thrills they have to offer;

- complicated, disorderly and disordered home situations that provide neither basis not roots. For many, school is their second home or even their first home.

It is all too easy to state that a good teacher can solve all these issues in class. And where, pray, are such superheroes to be found?

All these developments call for other spatial conditions and force one's thoughts towards a different type of school altogether.

In spatial terms, it is essential that the cramped patterns of thought still adhered to by school-builders should be abandoned in favour of more varied, more changeable and, most of all, more open space forms that incite greater concentration but also greater exchange, that give a more expansive view of the world. And it takes a lot more to achieve this than simply demolishing walls, leaving large open areas where everyone is a bother to everyone else.

We are just going to have to accept the idea of another kind of school, one that is less of an institution where you are robbed of your freedom, if only temporarily, and fed with knowledge. We need to look for a form of learning space with a wider range of experiences, as is found in the city and in the world of internet.

However exciting lessons are made, the computer screen contains a space whose mesmerizing power vies on a major scale with real space.[1] We can safely leave the business of discouraging children from straying into the space of the computer screen to educationalists. But if we are to be able to counterbalance the in-depth individual attention on screen, the space of the surroundings has to become all the more relevant, particularly as social space, if only to keep alive the reality of community. The one thing that can hold its own against the immaterial creatures on screen is real live girls and boys.

It is the presence of others that invests the school space with the most meaning – those of your own age and predicament that you have to work with and whom you may or may not feel drawn to. The others are your sounding board, your frame of reference, your fountain of inspiration. Being so mutually dependent, you need to come to terms with one another. You are condemned to each other's company in the great school that is society and your school building, besides providing spaces for reading, writing and arithmetic, must be tailored to this aspect too.

A school is then a single spatial entity with a key place given to social exchange. To this the so-called Extended Schools[2] add local facilities so that the whole comes ever closer to resembling a city, a micro-city.

The school for which we are to find a form is one of less education and more learning. What is needed is an environment that stimulates and incites learning by asking questions, a climate that provokes exchange and confrontation, intellectually, culturally and politically.

When study goes beyond the limits of so-called compulsory subject matter to become more, if not all-embracing, learning is no longer restricted by the classroom walls but will claim the entire space of the building. This will change the position and duty of teachers and pupils alike, creating new fields of responsibility which will need expressing in the school's spatial order.

Indeed, space is more than ever a means of showing pupils and especially teachers what the possibilities are, of inspiring them and opening itself up to changes and increments.

At all events, the building should not be a balanced, hermetic whole equipped simply for the objective at hand; it must be and remain accessible and essentially inviting, an appliance or rather an instrument for pupils, teachers and parents, one that can accept a change of contents and so continue functioning in changing situations.

1 From 'ik@nrc.nl', in NRC *Handelsblad*, 22-12-2005 (trans. JK):
REAL It was the 2005 trip to Rome, like every year for fifth- and sixth-formers at grammar school. We assembled in Bernini's arcade to visit St Peter's together. As we approached the cathedral* I heard a female pupil's voice behind me: "Hey, that square's much smaller than in reality!" I spun round to face her. "Do you know what you're saying?" I managed. To which she answered somewhat impatiently: "What I mean, of course, is – much smaller than on TV."
*Hubert Biezeveld*
* for cathedral read basilica
2 See Chapter 3, pp. 168-173

[1, 2] De Polygoon primary school
in Almere adapted for and by pupils
to make them feel at home

# Deschooling

A stimulating environment is an environment that appeals to you, that provokes you and incites you to act. For this you must be able to place the signals and stimuli it gives off – that is, make them part of a familiar domain. Learning is the process of making things part of your domain: making something that was once beyond you your own. This gives you a grip on your surroundings so that you acquire a place, and thus control over those surroundings.

The notion of school calls for an inner world that can give children confidence and security, that can feel familiar to them, like a house; an environment, then, that they can make their own.

The school building should arouse the right associations for this purpose. On no account should its functionality dominate or intimidate through associations with such institutes as hospitals, which are a nightmare for children, and preferably shouldn't involve either the overwhelmingly prominent constructivist high jinks architects are generally so fond of. Before anything else, the school has to resemble a residential building, as should every building where people spend time. Architecture cannot avoid a degree of detachment but should compensate for this by an ability to be coloured by personal hallmarks so that it can be appropriated.

This appropriation of space in schools is almost always marked by a generally chaotic-looking assemblage of stuff. Things the children have made stand and hang all over the place, blotting the building itself from view. It is difficult for an outsider to discern any order in this, an order that for those involved is unquestionably one of necessary and familiar resources and references. A tidy house may make for a tidy mind, but it is perhaps also restrictive and less likely to encourage activity.

This illustrates the importance of having convincing spatial leitmotifs to keep the

[1]

[2]

building palpable and visible throughout and without compromising the working conditions despite the fragmentation brought about by the variety and abundance of its contents.

The architect finds himself in a building quite unlike the one he had imagined, but where the intentions, the thinking behind it and the conditions for effective use are all the more prominent.

This is a sensitive issue, since few architects are prepared to see their product, their 'creation', submitted to the expression and expansiveness of such a seemingly unbridled excess of rampant forms and colours. It is largely for this reason that we, unlike those architects who reach for their box of paints mainly to be fashionable, have been exercising increasing restraint on the colouring front. The school colours itself. A confusing element is the misplaced contribution by industry which is all too keen to deliver its wares in a riot of colour, undoubtedly because they think that teachers think that children like it that way. Yet it is surely subtleties that make children aware of colour. We may treat the matter lightly but what we need besides another type of design is new ideas about the architect's role and the meaning of architecture in general.

The very act of designing a school requires renouncing the aesthetic we are familiar with and forces architects to shift the emphasis to another aesthetic, such as that of the city, where there always seems to be room for deviation, change and the unexpected. Indeed, variety in input is seen as a positive quality in a city and serves to confirm its spatial structure.

Schools today cannot escape the deschooling process. There is a greater or lesser shift in emphasis from obligatory schooling to more room for personal initiative and pleasure in learning. Hence the need for an environment more like that of a house, closer, less detached and more congenial.

As time goes by, we see the school building changing from an educational institute to a house of learning and, at the same time, a Learning City. This shifts the architect's focus to a domestic interior on the one hand and an urban interior on the other, in other words to those very domains beyond the control of the building's designer.

Architects, like urbanists, have to guarantee the spatial conditions for what could happen and what may be expected of it; *how* it will happen depends on the input of the users and the unfolding of their ideas over time.

An undeniable precursor of the 'New Learning' and the 'learning landscape' found everywhere these days is the Montessori method. Though it does retain the division into classrooms, these are populated by three successive 'years', so that each class essentially is a tiny school in itself. For the rest, the children fan out with unusual ease beyond their home base to seek out a place for their activities. But they do remain in the care of 'their' teacher on whom they can fall back and give an account of what they have been doing.

The 'New Learning' proceeds from much larger units and from teams of teachers often compounded in terms of particular subjects. It replaces the traditional teacher's desk with a 'help desk', a teacher station or enquiry counter where the children come for help and show their work, which is actually the way it has always been in a Montessori class. Schools are becoming more and more geared to accessibility, of means and resources and teachers alike. Everything has its place and is there for everyone. The new school is organized more as a city, a city of learning.

Apollo schools, Amsterdam

# The school appropriated

On revisiting our Polygoon School in Almere, built in 1990, we discovered it to be completely transformed. In those days form, material and colour were deliberately restrained to make the building easier to appropriate. And appropriated it was, and how! There are new bits added everywhere, undoubtedly meant to embellish it and give it an air of homeliness. All this goes to show just how much the stern, no-nonsense atmosphere we used to associate with learning, with only informative illustrations on the walls, has ceded to domesticity. Evidently what counts most nowadays is that the children feel at home and at ease and experience the school as a large house.

[1]

[2]

[3]

[4]

[5]

[6]

Everything that once made for a taut uncluttered background is now overrun with often entrancing illustrations, ornaments, decorations and all-pervading colours that scarcely leave any patch of surface uncovered. Is this powerful and exuberant response precisely because the architect deliberately left these areas blank? What is certain is that as a result the school was provoked into making its own decisions, and that a process of appropriation took place that would never have occurred had the colour planes been preprogrammed by the architect (although it isn't clear whether the children or the teachers did the appropriating).

◄ [1] Opened doors between
classrooms, De Eilanden
Montessori primary school,
Amsterdam

[2, 3] Working on individual carpets as temporarily appropriated
places, De Eilanden Montessori
primary school, Amsterdam

# Montessori

An element common to the orthodox 20th-century ideas on renewal in education –
Dalton, Jena Plan, Elmhurst, Steiner, Pestalozzi, Montessori – besides a new pedagogical
angle was that they broadened the traditional learning programme, mainly attuned as
this was to acquiring intellectual skills. In doing so, they opened up the school more to
the world.

Since we are concerned with the spatial consequences of these moves forward, we feel
justified in examining the Montessori system at this juncture. The Montessori method
seeks mainly to make the school more part of the world and therefore more accessible,
which undoubtedly ties in with its original aim of helping mentally retarded children.
This opening-up can be seen in the attempts to make the often abstract knowledge
children have to digest at regular schools more concrete, more applicable in practice
and more 'physical'. The much-misunderstood principle of free choice of purposeful
activity not only eradicates the force-feeding aspect but at the same time allows the
children to use their own enthusiasm, curiosity even, to drive their motivation. An
essential aspect here is the offering of options. This is where the Montessori system
sets itself far apart from all anti-authoritarian systems where it is left up to the children
to decide what to do.

This offer of a choice of paths to take is not restricted to the teacher's guiding suggestion
(what if you were now to do this, or that). In having the possibilities openly displayed,
it instils ideas in the pupils that they would not have had without the associations
evoked by making visible what is on offer. With three successive years brought together
in one room, the children also become acquainted with learning material originally
intended for those in a higher (or lower) group. Spatially this requires that everything
pupils are to make use of should be arranged openly and invitingly.

[2]

[3]

As everyone is occupied with their own work either alone or with others, this creates the ambience of a workshop, be it an untidy one at times, where what someone else is doing often seems more fun than your own activity.

Montessori schools began with regular classrooms, although these were incredibly large by our standards. These were modelled into zones like the rooms in a house, including a tiled wet area with a kitchen worktop and washbasins. Besides the more intellectual work, the Montessori system dwells at length on so-called domestic activities such as cleaning so that the children learn how to take care of their environment. With their own tablecloth and their own plant on their own little table, each child is encouraged to develop an awareness of and responsibility for their own territory. *Responsibility* Indeed, they can make a temporary place of their own for a particular self-chosen activity by rolling out pieces of carpet on an open patch of floor. The children have learned that it is inexcusable to encroach on places others have made for themselves.

In the modern Montessori school you see children working everywhere, outside the classrooms too; the school is itself a workshop with activity spilling out at every corner. Particularly 'cosmic education', learning targeted at the world and beyond, means magnifying and drawing in the world – which is where deschooling in education really begins.

[1]

[2]

[3]

## Attention and views

If there is little architects can add to the space of the traditional education paradigm with its firmest focus on instruction, the greater their field of activity when it concerns space for forms of learning that fall outside the well-trodden paths and where the children are entrusted with more responsibility. This requires quite another type of school building in which every association with obligation and restraints on freedom is absent. Rather, it is inviting and able to motivate and arouse curiosity among pupils who are distracted and unsettled by the over-the-top attractions of modern life.

The traditional programme of spaces wielded in briefs for school buildings, with rooms for teaching and learning (the net floor area) plus the 'necessary' circulation space, ancillary rooms and other areas falling outside the 'useful' working surface area, is utterly unsuited to modern education. The more emphasis shifts from instruction to learning, the more need there is for the opportunity for children to work either alone or with others in a group.

So the more nooks, corners and other out-of-the-way places the better. This calls for an articulated space where all opposition between net, useful space and additional, servant space dissolves and the notion of circulation space is irrelevant.

Instead you get a hybrid, delta-like cluster of islands where work is done. Those moving through the school do so between these islands, not along purposefully freed paths such as the traditional corridors, but more as if along paths in a landscape.

Modelling or articulating a space additionally means it can accept more activities. These activities should not be allowed to get in each other's way although they remain linked spatially. Whether you work alone or in a group, it requires a degree of isolation but not so much as to destroy the social unity of the whole. It is a question of finding a balance between conditions for concentrating and conditions for connectedness. The sense of belonging to a greater entity must be preserved.

Schools must be equipped for two fundamentally opposing conditions: on the one hand you should be able to concentrate (pupils' powers of concentration are generally not their strongest quality) and on the other an open system should be aspired to, one where you are together with the others and where there is much to see and do, where you can explore what the world has to offer and where your horizons are widened and your curiosity aroused. Yet such exhilarating and enticing things in such large supply will undoubtedly divert the attention.

This conflict between concentration and distraction by a welter of stimuli can only be resolved by spatial means. If education needs spatial responses anywhere, it is here; and this brings us to the most important task facing an architect designing a school. For here are the basic elements of architecture, namely views and 'cover', both of which should be present in a school building, side by side and in the right amounts. Schools must surely be the pre-eminent building type when it comes to these conditions.

[1] Seating on landing, De
Koperwiek primary school, Venlo

[2] Platform-block, Montessori
school, Delft

Different types of pedagogy, from traditional instruction to independent learning in all its facets, call for a wide range of spatial conditions that are bound to occur side by side. Today's school can therefore be seen as a conglomeration of space forms that are either introverted to some degree or extroverted.

Introverted places, call them centripetal, serve one's concentration whereas spaces that work centrifugally direct the attention outwards.

The space in a school, once consisting only of long corridors flanked by rows of hermetic classrooms, has been steadily evolving into a complex differentiation of open, less open and closed places of differing size and quality ranging from centralized attention to decentralization, to a whole host of centres of attention. In this new space, children and teachers alike have to discover, experience and understand what the world has to offer them and at the same time feel at home. This calls for an articulated space and requires of architects a creative endeavour hitherto unknown in the designing of schools. We shall have to abandon the traditional school building and take our inspiration from the city, as this too consists, if at a greater scale, of a changing pattern of qualities and a variety of places more or less separated physically but without forfeiting their social connections.

# Spatial conditions for attention and views

"Space should always be articulated in such a way that places are created, spatial units whose appropriate dimensions and correct measure of enclosedness enable them to accommodate the pattern of relations of those who will use it. How a space is articulated is a decisive factor: it will determine to a high degree whether the space will be suitable for a single large group of people, say, or for a number of small, separate groups. The more articulation there is the smaller the spatial unit will be, and the more centres of attention there are the more individualizing the overall effect becomes – that is, that several activities can be pursued by separate groups at the same time."[3]

So, a learning environment where wide-ranging activities can take place simultaneously and where groups and individuals can work independently, calls for the greatest number of places screened from one another in such a way that everyone can stay focused on their work, but at the same time offers a sufficiently clear view of others as to arouse each other's curiosity and give each other ideas and encouragement.

Spatial means are to bring about the conditions for independent (as opposed to classroom-based) learning situations. The space should be articulated so as to ensure conditions that strike the right balance between collective and individual actions as well as enlarging the potential capacity of workplaces. Our job and focus as architects is first and foremost to organize the space for this purpose:

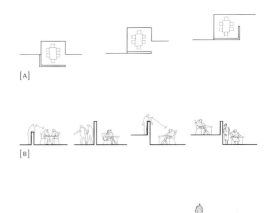

[A]

[B]

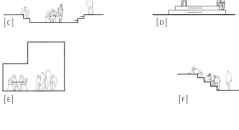

[C]  [D]

[E]  [F]

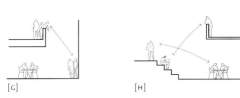

[G]  [H]

- by stressing the distinction between elongated street-like spaces with a through view and places more like rooms or nooks;
- by moving a workplace away from the line of fire to the sidelines, even if this means bending or shifting the flow of traffic [A];
- by dimensioning walls or partitions heightwise so that they separate or screen off visually and also acoustically [B];
- by differences in height, such as raising or lowering the floor in places as 'hollows' or 'islands' [C, D];
- by making differences in floor-to-ceiling height: taller areas are inevitably experienced as more collective and perhaps 'urban', whereas less-tall areas have a more intimate, protective feel [E];
- by making sitting-steps that act as a magnet at all times, bringing people together for each other and for events [F];
- by making openings in floors, voids that enable vertical views through and visually connect the storeys. Slipping floor surfaces out of alignment in split-level fashion creates a spatial continuum rather than a division of the building into horizontal slices [G, H];
- by siting inbuilt elements such as reading nooks, kitchen corners and teacher stations away from the periphery as autonomous islands marking and modelling the space. A corner primarily has an enclosing effect; it would be more central and attract more attention if it were moved from the sidelines to midspace. Freestanding wet cells, platforms and information desks are then islands that can be approached from all sides – mainstays in the open space [I];

- by being continually aware of sight lines created by the way the space is organized, lines that are evident in the plans and sections;

- by rationing the admission of daylight. This evokes the strongest associations with the streets and the city, particularly when daylight enters evenly and in an elongated form from above [J]. Light attracts people and encourages them to socialize. This is another reason why light concentrated at one point has a focusing effect [K]. If the quantity of light is comparatively easy to regulate, it is less simple for a designer to ascertain the architectural interventions that will bring about a particular *quality* of light. Thus light merely entering through roof openings or high sidelights is always sadly lacking, whereas lateral reflecting surfaces unfailingly bring a light source to life [L, M];

- by providing clear contrasts between light and dark, for example by rationing local concentrations of artificial light. A lamp above a table marks out a field of attention and is a powerful placemaker, picking out this field from its surroundings;

- by rationing the sound in a space, the acoustics. Sound like vision is a form of perception and audibility gives an indication of collective endeavour. Sound is experienced as engaging or disturbing, depending on the situation. It is best not to hear too much of the activity around you if you want to concentrate. By regulating the acoustics in a space, the sense of individuality and intimacy is strengthened and distinguished from the collective. Too much sound reduction stifles the sense of community. Wall-to-wall carpeting muffles not only the sound but also the effect of children's movements. They are unaware that they are stamping or indulging in other boorish behaviour. They will fail to learn to keep their motor behaviour under control, as the effects of colliding with each other are less up front and therefore less conspicuous;

[1]

- by juxtaposing different materials for purposes of articulation and place identification. Materials arouse particular associations that can influence the way places are used. Thus, for instance, wooden steps will sooner bring to mind a table than would stone steps, aside from the fact that wood is more comfortable to work on than cold stone. Sustainability is another factor. Material that is impossible to damage will not teach children to treat it with respect and to recognize what you can and cannot do with it;

- by covering parts of the floor with carpeting to distinguish them as places, thereby articulating the floor area as a whole. The local use of warmer, more touchy-feely materials denotes quality of place or 'placeness'.

3 *Lessons for Students in Architecture*, p. 193

# Steps

Space can be articulated by raising or lowering sections of floor. It is important to give particular thought to the transitions, designing these wherever possible as tiers of seating with intervening steps in places where stairs are required.

Steps mark a transition between two areas, not as a hard line between them but as a area in its own right. You might call it a threshold area.

Steps can both open up views and give protection. They therefore satisfy the conditions for a place that not only attracts people but manages to keep them there. They will become hangout areas, as required by children of all ages and in all circumstances, places that provide certainty in an excessively open and uncertain world. Steps can also be interpreted as long worktops. Like the rugs or pieces of carpet in the Montessori tradition you can lay out your stuff in comparative safety without it being trampled. If the rugs are temporary mobile territories, steps, through the conditions they create, arouse a sense of place that easily lends itself to work. The association with a table is strengthened by the fact that they are of wood. And if you see children tending to take off their shoes to work there, they are simply obeying the hard-and-fast rule 'no shoes on the table'.

Wherever these sitting-steps bridge differences in height of a storey or half-storey, there emerges a kind of theatre that encourages spontaneous activity as well as providing seats for presentations without the need to drag chairs around. Evidently, children who may be just hanging out or waiting often need the slightest pretext to indulge in spontaneous play-acting, with the surrounding rudiments of a theatre creating a situation of audience and performers in the shortest time.

[2]

[3]

The generally awkward space under the bottom of most stairs can be accessed and
used when the floor area here is made deeper. This gives a sheltered nook away from
the toing and froing and with an element of intimacy; a desirable spot for one or a few
pupils to withdraw to, where they can read or be alone for a while. Schools should
have many more such places. Similarly, the gap below steps contains much potential
storage space, even if only for stacking cushions to sit on.

Steps and sunken spots activate the floor as a work area. It transpires that there are
many activities where children prefer working on the floor. This is made clear enough
by the Montessori rugs, which are much larger than the customary tables, though
there are times when the lack of a fixed limit to one's field of attention may lead to
other, more informal behaviour.

[1]

[2]

# Built furniture as anchors

[1-4] Apollo schools, Amsterdam

[5, 6] De Evenaar primary school, Amsterdam

[7-9] De Salamander, Arnhem

Kitchen corners, worktops for reading or for computers, library units, teachers' stations, nooks for sitting and working, platforms and other places for particularized activities are preferably pushed against walls or tucked into them as niches so as not to be in the way and take up as little space as possible. Stand them freely midspace and they become islands, 'built' furniture resembling small houses that can be approached from all sides. This gives you objects in space, built structures that divide up and so

[1]

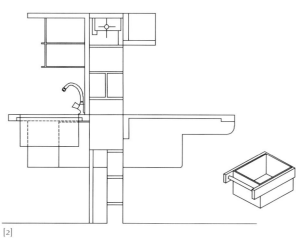

[2]

[3]

[4]

[5]

[6]

articulate the space around them. They make the space smaller and larger at the same time: smaller because the intervening areas are reduced, larger because the overview is made multiple. They mediate, so to speak, between furniture and rooms. (This is why a room with furniture in it looks bigger than when empty.)

This 'built' furniture compels attention, detached as it is from the periphery of the surrounding space which fades into the background. The space then becomes more exterior and more city-like in relation to the smaller spatial units placed in it. Objects in space have a structuring effect though without dividing that space into detached units, the way walls do. Freestanding elements become anchors, if you like, hubs of

[7]

[8]

[9]

activity. As centres, they have a space-defining, magnetizing effect. You can push things against them, tables for instance, that then look less lost and more defined in the space, but they can also fulfil a circumscribing role. They are open to whatever gets pushed against them and to whatever is to be bounded and screened off.

The fireplace that was once part of the handicrafts room of the Delft Montessori School has vanished during internal alterations, for reasons that are anything but clear. In all likelihood objections such as dust and danger gained the upper hand over the adventure of baking clay figures or bread and playing with fire, just as the gully outside (see page 184) has fallen into disuse through practical objections. And yet fire and water have a right to be there too, for all the objections and risks attached to them. An open fire in particular has its attractions and is a natural centre you can sit round, confirming the idea of a school as a house.

[2]

[3]

# Block and hollow

"The central point of the hall in the Delft Montessori School is the brick platform-block, which is used for both formal assemblies and spontaneous gatherings. At first sight it would seem that the potential of the space would be greater if the block could be moved out of the way from time to time and, as was to be expected this was indeed a point of lengthy discussions. It is the permanence, the immobility, and the 'being in the way' that is the central issue, because it is indeed that inescapable presence as a focal point that contains the suggestions and incentives for response in each situation as it arises. The block becomes a 'touchstone' and contributes to the articulation of the space in such a way that the range of possibilities of usage increases.

"In each situation the raised platform evokes a particular image and since it permits a variety of interpretations, it can play a variety of different roles. The children use it to sit on or to lay out materials during handwork classes, music lessons and all the other activities which take place in the school hall. They are themselves stimulated to take on a greater variety of roles.

"Incidentally, the platform can be extended in all directions with a set of wooden sections, which can be drawn out from the interior of the block to turn it into a real stage for actual theatre, dance and music performances. The children can put the different parts together and take them apart again themselves, without help from the teacher. During the lunch breaks the children play games on and around it, or they huddle together there to look at their picture books when there is in fact plenty of space all around them. To them it is an island in a sea of shiny floor-space.

"The floor in the hall of the kindergarten section has a square depression in the mid-

[2]

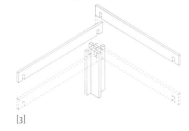

[3]

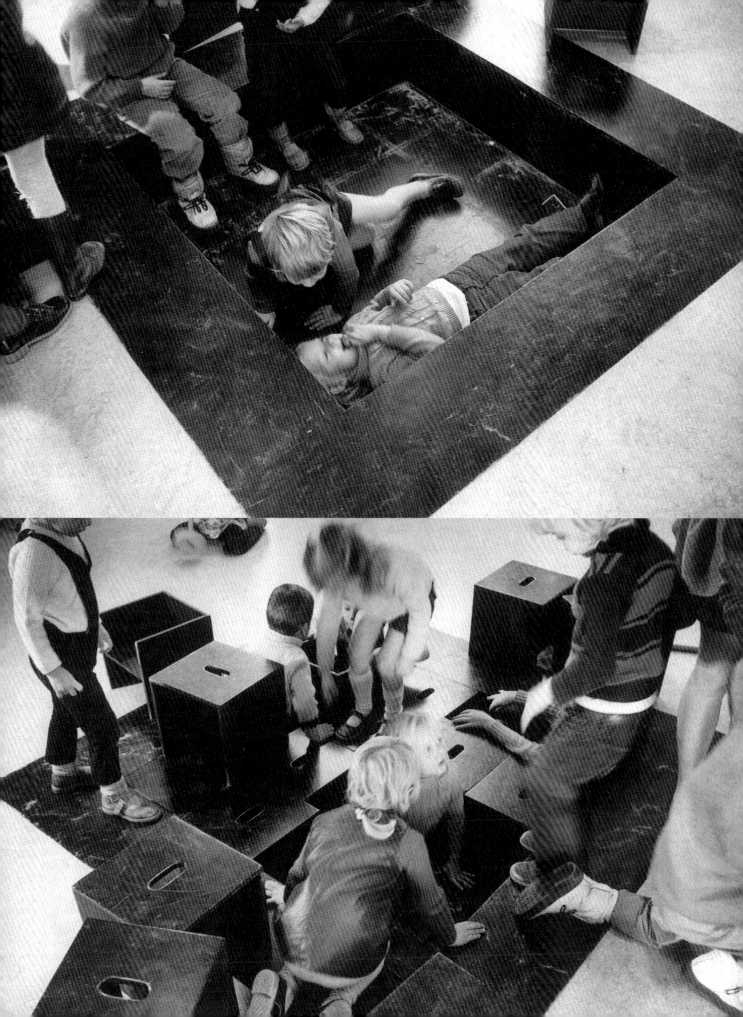

dle which is filled with loose wooden blocks. These can be taken out and placed around the square to form a self-contained seating arrangement. The blocks are constructed as low stools, which can easily be moved by the children all around the hall, or they can be piled up to form a tower. The children also use them to make trains. In many respects the square is the opposite of the brick platform in the other hall. Just as the block evokes images and associations with climbing a hill to get a better view, so the square gives a feeling of seclusion, a retreat, and evokes associations with descending into a valley or hollow. If the platform-block is an island in the sea, the hollow square is a lake, which the children have turned into a swimming pool by adding a diving board."[4]

Platform-block and sitting-hollow are not just opposites, they are complementary as well. The hollow is more introverted, the block is a safe place too but more outward-facing. A platform can be a plinth, a table, a pedestal, with something exultant about it; you're on show, at the centre, attracting all the attention. In the hollow, by contrast, you hide from view. Both attributes, platform-block and sitting-hollow (the same size in this case), focus the attention and are centres and assembly points for inciting shared activity. You can address bystanders from the platform and enjoy the intimacy of the hollow for a chat or to be read a story in a group.

4 Adapted from *Lessons for Students in Architecture*, pp. 153-154

[1]

[2]

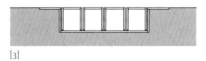

[3]

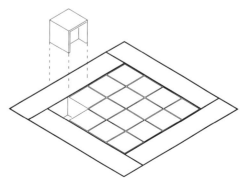

[4]

[5]

# The space of place

Places for learning situations need to strike the right balance between 'cover' and views out and therefore be inviting, creating an active working atmosphere and thus the spatial conditions to keep a group together. Pictures, books, plants, learning material and of course the projects the pupils themselves make have their own galvanizing effect. A logical next step is to openly present the available study material, so that all can clearly see what is on offer.

Ethnologists and primatologists are continually hammering at the importance of the quality of the environment for mental development.[5] We are always hearing about the importance of a rich environment for growing animals and how their intellectual development depends on it. There is no reason to suppose that it is any different for children, and maybe to an even stronger degree.

By rich environment is meant an environment of change, of exhilarating experiences and opportunities for discovery; an environment rich in positive stimuli and above all where a social life is enacted. We can surely then assume that the same demands – that an environment should energize and incite – should be made of a school, an environment meant primarily for learning.

A further condition for a learning situation is that it holds out the possibility of appropriating that environment as a familiar and safe zone, so that work becomes more part of normal daily life, inclusive and with a natural feel to it.

What we need to do is deploy spatial means that spawn a challenging environment that is at the same time familiar territory. At first glance, these two conditions seem contradictory since to challenge presupposes the surprise of change and unexpected situations, whereas familiar territory should be constant and readily identifiable. The learning environment should resemble a city that is continually changing because houses change and shops get refitted, but where the streets are the same familiar streets. The overall structure stays the same even if its texture changes.

In a school design, then, the floors and walls should have a containing capacity that allows the content to change without affecting the whole. Walls should in fact be nothing other than cupboards with open compartments that are unfazed by changes in use.

An environment that is able to absorb the images and things we like having around us so that we can engage with them needs to possess an accumulative capacity. Place-making is facilitated by a familiar and at the same time challenging environment: the space of place.

"Architects should on the whole try to make objects more substantial, less two-dimensional – by thinking more in terms of zones. Freestanding walls, if they don't reach the ceiling and are sufficiently thick, can serve as shelves for putting things on. One of the striking things about Italian churches in particular is that they have a knee-high projecting stone plinth running round much of the wall, on which you will always see people sitting or lying. And the motorcars of the old days had running boards to facilitate getting in and out, which also made excellent extra seats during a picnic. The extension of the usable space by the addition of (informal) extra horizontal planes

[3]

[4]

[5]

[3-4] Apollo schools, Amsterdam

◄ [1, 5] De Evenaar primary school, Amsterdam

[2] De Spil Extended School, Arnhem

represents the reward for making more explicit what was in fact an implicit requirement. And if this added value is seen primarily as yielding an enlargement of the capacity for seating and for putting things on, this may seem a somewhat limited advantage at first sight. But the point here is the designer's or architect's commitment (both in general and in particular) to create this added value wherever possible, as the users will turn such extras to further advantage. Such intensification of the material should, ideally, become second nature to the architect, a question of handwriting rather than an extra, less a matter of what you design than of how you design it."[6]

To design what we build more as a 'zone' is to build it more substantially, in other words less flat as if of cardboard and more as a volume so that it has the capacity to contain. It means that you must transcend the bare programme calculated to the nearest cent and based on a few cramped duties. And it is this dimension that is the first to suffer from squeezed budgets that step off from performance at its most stripped-down. We are talking about 'the space of form'.[7] This means that walls, floors and ceilings don't serve exclusively as elements of separation but are able to contain and therefore give substance and meaning.

By taking up the capacity to contain as an explicit quality in what is built, its users (teachers, pupils, enlightened parents) are invited, or even incited, to engage with the building in some way. It is this very challenge, which differs according to circumstances, that will lead on each new occasion to a multi-coloured variety of infills.

An environment that is to create the conditions for learning has to be able to accept the most varied contents within the intimacy of the place; learning requires that you have the whole world around you. Shelves, compartments, nooks, ledges and walls doubling as cupboards help you to frame things so that each acquires value in itself and will command attention, while at the same time there is clarity of organization, because everything has a place and stays there rather than drifting about. Flexibility requires thin partitions, lightweight structures, a minimum of material and fugitive qualities.

The capacity to contain calls for thickness, or rather depth. Which is why everything we make – floors, walls, window and door frames – requires volume.

Amenities such as cloakroom corners, display cases, widened shelves above doors and on window frames, raised additional window ledges, built-on cupboards, study niches, window worktops, kitchen recesses or islands – all these see to it that everything gets its own recognizable place, establishing a degree of clarity in an otherwise dense fog of attributes and eventualities.

People and things require nooks and crannies to inhabit in space. An essential quality in this respect is what we might call 'cupboardness', with the kangaroo as our ideal.[8]

Buildings must be open to change, which in the case of schools means being tuned to new pedagogical insights. However, when we architects fail to adopt a clear position due to doubt and uncertainty, what remains of the building is spineless, bare, emaciated. And then we will have only done the financing authorities a favour, convinced as they were already that it was costing far too much. There is, regrettably, a misconception that persists among architects regarding the slogan 'Less is more', which when taken at face value suggests that it is best to do as little as possible. But there is a difference between reducing and concentrating. Instead of leaving out essential elements,

[1]

[2]

[3]

[4]

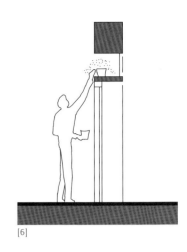

[6]

[7]

[8]

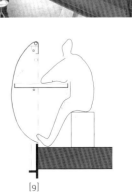

[9]

[5]

[1]

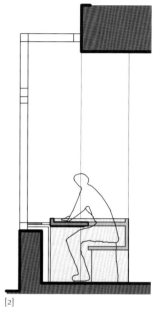

[2]

[3]

[4]

[5]

[6]

[7]

we must try to arrive at the essence, a concentration, just as poets restrict themselves to just those words in just that order that together pack the greatest punch. This results in what we once named polyvalence, that is, limiting yourself to forms that are continually able to take up a different content and a new meaning while remaining themselves, and so in principle never change.[9] It's all down to the form's capacity or 'competence' to remain useful and meaningful in different circumstances. You can't create a learning environment with flexibility. Children need to be able to rely on their environment if they are to be receptive to new experiences, and the restrictions of the traditional classroom offered them that. The challenge here is that the modern school with its freedom of choice has to be like a city but at the same time like a house. In other words, a school must be like a city where you can feel at home. The complexity of this task is typical of architecture and nowhere as sensitively expressed as in the designing of schools today.

5  See *Forum van architectuur en daarmee verbonden kunsten*, no. 3, 1962: Flexibiliteit en polyvalentie
6  Adapted from *Lessons for Students in Architecture*, p. 188
7  See *Lessons for Students in Architecture*, pp. 150-151
8  A reference to Gaston Bachelard, *La poétique de l'espace*, Paris: Presses Universitaires de France, 1957. Translated as *The Poetics of Space* (Boston: Beacon Press, 1969/1994)
9  See *Lessons for Students in Architecture*, p. 147

[1]

[2]

# Articulation and whole

By articulating a space, you can make distinctions in conditions. You can distinguish between spatial qualities for a diversity of uses, so that pupils in different group forms with different learning resources are able to concentrate on a wide range of subjects. To articulate in fact means to fragment into smaller units which are able to take on their own distinguishable properties and qualities, resulting in an increase in complexity and with it the risk of clouding the issue. Not just that, this abundance and diversity of more individual learning situations in tune with the new education is itself subject to change.

If pupils run the risk of getting lost in an excessively big and seemingly chaotic world, the important thing for teachers is to keep it all under control without being too much in evidence.

The more children work individually and the more the space they work in is tailored to these conditions by being articulated into smaller units, the greater the need to retain a clear overview of the whole. And what architecture has to do is to secure a visual unity that manages to draw together spatially the many parts from which the whole is assembled.

There comes a time when you can't see the woods for the trees, when you lose your grasp of the whole as much logistically as visually. This is a phenomenon we know from music, where misplaced emphasis can undermine the natural flow of the piece and reduce it to a succession of fragments. There are many public buildings where you soon lose sight of the whole when spatial cohesion is subordinated to the many components jostling for attention, such as at most airports, in libraries and in supermarkets. You are then left at the mercy of printed coded signage and this is not always easy to read. Unable to get your bearings, you feel as if lost in a labyrinth, which is what many buildings are like.

This is why articulation needs to be kept in balance by an underlying principle that ensures that the whole hangs together, an inclusive frame that gives an overview of and perspective on the space and the educational package on offer there.

Articulation requires the foil of a spatial overview, that the whole exhibits a clear, city-like order.

A school building should derive its clarity of organization from a spatial structure that encapsulates the complexity of the entire building, its horizon as it were.

We expect the spatial structure to endure, even when its contents are modified. So the look of the parts can change but the essential factors defining the structural frame can not.

What we call structure is that aspect of a building that remains after it has been emptied, for instance when a new organization with new spatial claims makes its entrance. The spatial structure remains and is universally applicable, sustainable and above all else connective and secures the cohesion of the whole. Just this makes it possible to create within it a great number of places and islands of attention and concentration. But one should also bear in mind that the need may present itself for a return to larger space units, classrooms for instance.

Whatever the procedures of learning and how these work in time, differently for each

individual no doubt, what is certain is that it all hinges on the structuredness of, and familiarity with, the environment. And this is where architecture provides the not unimportant condition of an environment attuned to learning. This environment needs a degree of stability, so it should not be rooted in uncertainty. However, given the need for flexibility, that is, the opportunity to be able to change, the uncertainty factor is all too quick to assert itself. It is impossible to imagine our lives, and indeed the design process, without change and changeability. But this only creates all the more need for a stable framework to capture that changeability so that we don't lose control over the connectedness of the whole and the place of the constituent components within it.

There is enough upheaval as it is with the unceasing modifications to educational renewal and the march of new projects, to say nothing of school extensions and the reorganization these require. If you want children to feel sufficiently at home and regard the school as a familiar world, this is reason enough to strive for a stable spatial structure able to take up change without changing itself.

The spatial structure, the horizon of the building as a whole, has to tie together everyone engaged inside, but should also be a summary of all the learning possibilities on offer there and thus achieve a social as much as an educational unity.
In a school, the emphasis must be on the visual links between the different learning situations, as a single spatial network, comparable with the city, held together by a system of streets and squares or, like the brain, a network of paths linking the various centres.
Just as the brain functions not as a storehouse of knowledge but as a network of paths threading all knowledge together, you can regard the workings of an educational building as that of a brain, as a unit with many centres, which though sealed in themselves have the greatest possible openness towards one another.

◄ [1]  Gully in playground (since demolished), Montessori school, Delft

# 3 The School
# as a Micro-City

# Learning street

There are school buildings where learning and instruction are not confined to the class-rooms, where there is as much going on outside the classrooms as inside, and where there are no longer corridors as such with coats hanging everywhere and bags and rucksacks scattered around. What was originally a space for passing through is now a place to stay. So it is important to design this zone so as to encourage the greatest number and variety of places where you can work alone, in pairs or in a larger group, attentively and without being unduly distracted. These places have to have a high visibility, encouraging others to join you there and either join in or engage in their own activity. Workplaces then should enjoy a degree of protection and cover, but at the same time be open enough for you to see and to be seen by others. To achieve this balance between spatial conditions is, accordingly, the most important task facing the architect.

Aside from the space allocations specified in the programme, which need not specifically require enclosed spaces and are often used only part of the time, the main issue is to make as many unallocated workplaces or corners, giving cause to stay if only briefly. This inviting quality soon calls for extra space, at all events more space than would be the bare minimum for circulation alone. It does give you additional study space in return, be it beyond the classrooms.

[2]

What were once straightforward circulation passages are transformed into a true learning area where you can walk as well as work and where passers-by may get drawn to the workers without disturbing them. Here, it is the spatial qualities more than anything else that determine whether you feel at home or lost and whether you are encouraged to further explore the world you find yourself in.

By moving through the school, you should become part of what the others are engaged in and eligible for the package of possibilities there is to choose from. This should arouse your curiosity and give you ideas.

The wider the supply on offer, the more the school is a model of the world that children can grasp. This makes a journey through the school an educational promenade, by analogy with the *promenade architecturale* Le Corbusier must have envisaged when he thought of the succession of experiences gained when you move through a space with its changes in lighting, views, vistas, height and colour.

► p. 117

[1]

[2]

[3]

[4]

# Educational promenade, Montessori School, Delft, 1960-1966

After repeated extensions, the Montessori School in Delft developed to such a size and extent that it took an age to walk through, so that a separate entrance in the newest part for the youngest groups seemed necessary. Although the internal link was retained, this would remain a fairly secondary short-cut as it led through various subject rooms.

With this second entrance, the younger children could make their way directly into the part of the school intended for them without having to mix with the older ones. And yet the second entrance was abandoned quite early on, with no hope of reopening. The school's director, Rien Brederode, explained that on reflection

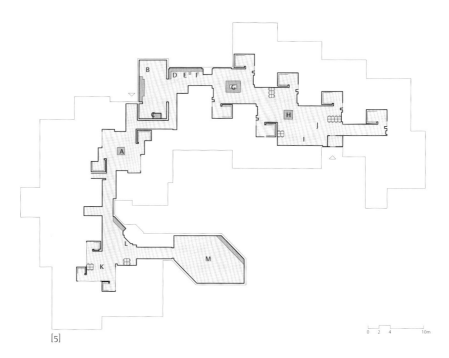

[5]

0  2  4       10m

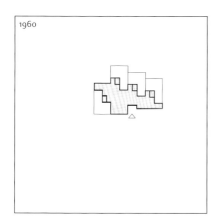

1960

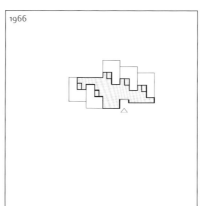

1966

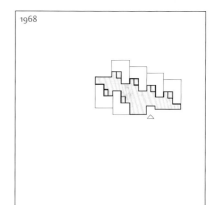

1968

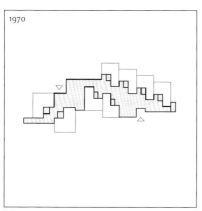

1970

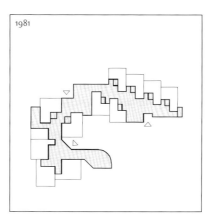

1981

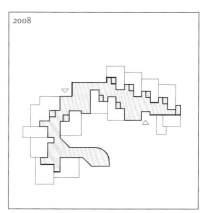

2008

[6]

[1] 'Square', Montessori school, Delft (photo from the 1980s)

[2] Ground floor 'square', Montessori College Oost, Amsterdam

he thought it better that the children, and particularly the youngest, should each day get an overview of the activities in the school before setting to work; that walking past classrooms, through the library, past the bee-keeping project, by way of the handicraft and other projects being worked on in all corners of the communal central area, they would drink in all the possibilities and take note of what they could expect in the future.

So every day all the children get a cross-section of all the learning opportunities available at the school, an educational promenade if ever there was one.
That the enlargement would lead bit by bit to a conglomeration, with the 'high street' zigzagging its way through it, was inevitable. It has created places by the score, but the clarity of organization has suffered as a result.

[1]

[2]

**[Learning street (continued)]**

In the classroom, you all know each other and are part of a group that often has something of a large family. Whenever classrooms open up more to the common central area and the work zone shifts and expands, the children have more dealings with others from other groups. Different ages get mixed together giving a richer and more complex social pattern in which everyone has to find their niche as best they can, and learn to function as one of many without being dominated or ignored. This confrontation with others, through which you come to understand how to get along with them, is perhaps as important as language and arithmetic. Familiarizing yourself with the world, being educated in living with others and thus in being independent, is an increasingly important learning process that unquestionably belongs at school, alongside obtaining knowledge and understanding. School then is a training ground for community and belonging. In a multicultural society where people think along different lines and family situations are becoming looser, with children raised to less explicit values and standards, there is an increasing need to make your intentions understood, both in and out of school. This is why you must learn to listen to each other, negotiate, mediate, make sacrifices, confer, return, redress, admit, stand firm, meet, make peace, console.

How can we turn the compact and limited bastion that is school into the most complete possible world for the 'untrained', where children are confronted with a high-powered magnification of their experience, where in all their vulnerability, security and adventure must balance each other out? The least we can expect of architecture is that it should help to keep that magnification of experience focused.

If we are to prepare children for the environment they occupy and familiarize them with it, that environment has to be much more than a space that looks good to the architect. The school has to most basically encompass and reflect the world in its wealth of aspects, mentalities and potentials, but in such a shielded environment that it can be kept legible and inclusive and guided by the teaching staff. Just this makes it a training ground for society.

The quality of the space is not a given in itself but gains expression through the people populating it and the acts it incites from them. When not in use, the building is nothing more than an empty shell. Architecture ought to follow and support the situations of people in their relationships with each other, their movements and what it is that moves them. In other words, those populating the space should find their true selves in relation to one another. Only this can give architecture its splendour.

If the influence of the design of the spatial order is anywhere of consequence, then it is in the creating of conditions; it works as a catalyst for contact and exchange. Architecture influences the way we deal with each other, and the design of a school can therefore influence relational skills. This is not only part of education in the broadest sense of the word, it strengthens the cohesion within the school population.

► p. 123

[1]

# Work balconies, Montessori College Oost, Amsterdam, 1993-1999

Halfway along the elongated voids between the front and rear parts of the building with their floors shifted a half-storey, are a number of work balconies that reduce the difference in height between floors to a quarter of a storey. Doubling as stairs, they are aligned in such a way that they and the stairs alongside them present a route spanning the entire height of the building. Each balcony has a landing and is the right shape and size to accept a table. This is another place suitable for giving lessons to a group, sitting on the double-height steps. In practice these balconies are usually used as a place to meet and hang out, where different groups are found together, more or less screened off by the high-rising side panels.

The balconies are necessary to break up and articulate the more than 90-metre-long galleries, acting as a series of small plazas that make the space easy to read and conducive to spending time there. They derive in principle from the stepped hall of the Apollo Schools, which also bridges a half-storey. Here at the much larger Montessori College Oost this is repeated seven times, giving rise to a whole host of centres.

[1]

[2]

[3]

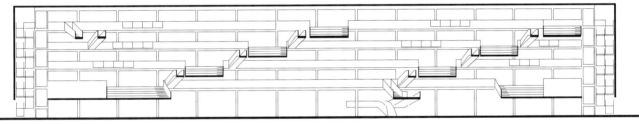

[4]

[4] Longitudinal section through work balconies

[5] Reference: Apollo schools, Amsterdam

[6] Cross section through work balcony

[5]

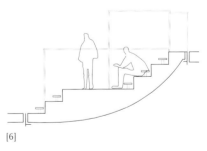

[6]

[Learning street (continued)]

The more extensive the building, the more alert you have to be not to lapse into laby-
rinths of excessively long and dark networks of passages where you pass each other by
with no hope of contact, let alone actually meeting. You then tend to go your separate
ways in a fog of anonymity. Worse still, if it is impossible to avoid the compartmenta-
tion and doors required by fire safety regulations, the building gets split up and gone
is the sorely needed spatial cohesion.

A first requirement is to do everything that can strengthen the spatial unity, and
everything that brings overall clarity of organization. Even when the client, out of a
fear of the monolithic, insists on dividing up the building into autonomous smaller
units, it is all the more necessary to find means of tying these units together spatially
so that they are experienced as a coherent whole, comparable with neighbourhoods
and urban quarters tied together by arterial roads and constituting an entity accessible
to all. With a lucid network of streets stitching it all together, you keep feeling that
cohesion as you cross the city with its neighbourhoods of different character.

Every educational building calls for a spatial order that works as a structure of streets
and squares together forming a small city where everything is geared to the greatest
possible number of social contacts, confrontations, meetings, adventures and discoveries. In other words, you are faced with a wider world that includes not just those of
your own age. Besides articulating the space so that a welter of learning activities can
function side by side, our concern here is to strengthen and incite social relations
using spatial means. Rendered in spatial terms, it basically means a building that can
enable an array of visual relations.

At secondary schools in particular, visual relationships are all-important. When the
mutual interest between boys and girls takes over and infatuations begin to seem more
than just that, keeping an eye on each other is all-important. This is an additional reason for not hiding the daily movement through the school in corridors and closed-off

[2]

stairwells but instead making it as central and as open as possible, a high street through the building where you cross each other's paths at random or by design. You can organize space in such a way that it can bring or keep people together, much like an electromagnetic field. You have to have a connection of some sort to feel a sense of belonging together. So you must be able to see and be seen by each other.

There are a number of spatial means that can be used to make a building a social or relational entity:

1 By tying its storeys together visually you prevent the building from being divided up by floors into horizontal layers. Voids, designed deliberately to promote visual relationships, make the building a spatial entity and prevent it from seemingly and ineluctably breaking up into isolated departments. A split-level division, for example, gives continuity between storeys, and voids, if their form and dimensions permit good sight lines, will make the space taller. A void can break through the oppressive standard storey height. By making corridors taller, their overall importance is enhanced and they become more street-like, an effect strengthened considerably by having them toplit with natural light, suggesting an outdoor space.

2 By projecting through the building the most lucid possible network of open indoor spaces, which aside from the overall clarity of organization it brings, acts as the main connecting artery of internal circulation. So rather than hiding the internal traffic, it makes it visible for everyone.

3 By making mobility in the building visible, for example by not hiding stairs but showing them openly and from all sides. Those moving through it then become the focus of attention.

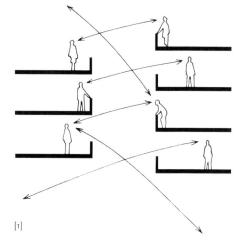

[1]

So we see the innards of the school no longer consisting of a maze or rabbit warren of variously-sized passages between variously-sized hermetic rooms but as a spatial whole tuned to social life by giving views of others and the experiences and lessons these can provide.

The closer we get to the essential conditions of the open learning environment, the closer we come to the paradigm of the city. In this situation classrooms, the least open components of a school, resemble houses in the urban elevations of streets and squares.

If classrooms are relatively static as home bases, the space beyond them has developed from the traditional corridor into something like an educational shopping street, an environment for learning in the widest sense of the word – a learning street.

The components traditionally described as dedicated – lunch and stayover room, library, assembly hall, gymnasium – are steadily opening up and being absorbed by the large area at the school's core. If articulated properly, these functions overlap rather than exist side by side. This central space is also able to house a wide range of additional activities previously excluded due to lack of space.

It is here in the Netherlands, where there is no money for separate rooms for art, music and drama, that this relatively extensive central space holds out possibilities. In the learning street there is room for exhibitions, presentations, performances, computer stations, corners for playing chess and draughts, table tennis tables, places for video instruction, pets care and observation posts, retail facilities. In fact, all enterprises where the whole school is to be involved take place in the central area beyond the

[2]

[3] ►

[1]

classrooms. Incontestably, the success of these activities hinges on whether the build-ing is spatially conducive to them.

All this transforms the school from a rigid constellation of isolated hermetic units into an open mosaic of overlapping, shifting activities. When integrated with such urban features as a library, crèche, pre-schoolers' playroom, before- and after-school facilities, and sports and community resources, schools become sociocultural centres, forfeiting their autonomy in the process and together becoming a city: a micro-city.

# The school building as a micro-city

When designing a school, you should be thinking all the time of a city and drawing parallels with urban situations though without lapsing into too literal analogies. Cities are too diffuse for that and their imagery too complex. Should you succeed in regarding your building as a tiny city, you will come to interpret the different components in another way.

"In the design phase, once this 'connection' has been made, a train of further associations is released, adding a new dimension to the quality of the communal, 'public'

[2]

places. Corridors become 'streets', interior lighting becomes 'street lighting' and so on. Although a building can never be a city nor anything between the two, it can still become city-like and thus become a better house.

"This reciprocal house-city image leads to a consistent articulation of large and small both inside and outside in sequences of contingent units which interlock without stress or effort. When this articulation is carried through to the smallest dimension, not only buildings and cities acquire reciprocal meaning, but buildings and furniture also, because large scale pieces of 'built' furniture are like small houses in which one feels yet more interiorized than in a large room. Thus each part is given the dimension which suits its purpose best, i.e. the right size through which it comes into its own."[1]

If it is possible to interpret buildings as small cities, then school buildings must be the best example by far. A central common area, surrounded and shaped by a periphery of more hermetic entities, classrooms, unmistakably calls to mind the image of a public space of street or square alongside a more private built zone. Indeed, the school community probably acts more like an urban community than that of most other buildings; as a social unit with a certain connectedness or feeling of belonging together, comparable perhaps with some neighbourhoods.

At school the emphasis is on social space, an open and clearly organized system where all the attributes of learning and thinking are readily accessible. So the school could well be illustrative of another type of public space than that of today's cities, eroded as they are by feelings of aloofness and inhospitality.

However, it is not just that our image of the school can learn from the city and its essentially social condition; the school in turn endows the city with the image of an instructive space, a public domain rich in meaning and therefore a wellspring of experiences. Ultimately, the school can be seen as a model of the world.

Just this association with schools as the new paradigm gives us an idea of how we should deal with urban public space, the pre-eminent place to express a sense of collectivity, despite all the traffic, and to generate social space, at least locally and if only as islands in the city.

1 Herman Hertzberger, 'The mechanism of the twentieth century
   and the architecture of Aldo van Eyck', in *Aldo van Eyck*, Amsterdam: Stichting Wonen, 1982, p. 12

# Street and square

All forms of space in cities that succeed in drawing people together and holding them there, and thus have a centripetal effect, can be reduced to either a street or a square. Square and street are the two basic forms of centralizing, relational space; heart and main artery if you like. Both can, in their own way, be the centre of a city or quarter as centre of gravity and median respectively, but just as easily the centre of a building. However many variations, intermediate forms and hybrids there are, at the end of the day it is still a square or a street.

In every city, even when laid out along egalitarian lines, main arteries or squares will take shape sooner or later as the centre whose surroundings will then turn to face. This centre can take the form of high streets as well as squares, or the two combined.

The street owes its role as centre to conditions quite unlike those of the square. The city square is brought out to full effect by special events that attract throngs of people. This soon makes it the spatial symbol of community, though the square itself may not be able to hold the entire city population. The main street can only perform this duty in exceptional cases, say for a parade, procession or demonstration and on rare occasions as the most elongated of squares. Piazza Navona in Rome and Piazza delle Erbe in Verona, long though they are, still behave like squares, although more than one centre can form there.

In any street space you walk through, the emphasis lies on the chance encounter (think of the Ramblas in Barcelona, La Canebière in Marseille or Placa in Dubrovnik), not that this was ever really the intention. In a square by contrast, a dedicated place at the juncture of several streets, encounters have a more deliberate aspect. A square is

[1]

[2]

[1]

[2]

[3]

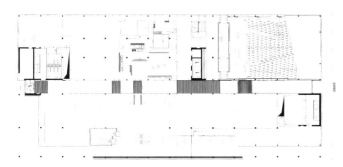
[4]

[5]

[6]

[7]

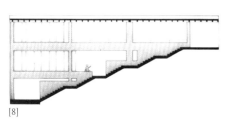
[8]

[9]

[10]

[1] 'Celebrating Queen Victoria's Jubilee', residential street in Saxmundham, England in 1887

[2] Rockefeller Center, New York, USA

[3] Sandpit, Montessori school, Delft

[4-7] Erick van Egeraat, InHolland University of Applied Sciences, Rotterdam, 1996-2000

[8-10] MBM Arquitectes, Thau School, Barcelona, Spain, 1972-1975

[11, 12] DOK Architecten, De Kikker Extended School, Amsterdam, 2000-2006

[13-15] Architectenbureau Marlies Rohmer, Terwesten Primary School, The Hague, 2001-2005. Playroom as central school hall for a variety of uses

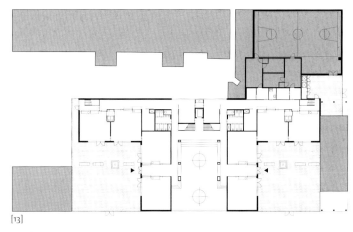

[13]

[14]

[11]

[15]

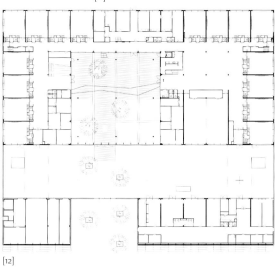

[12]

something you make your way to, that you converge on; it is a form that automatically incites such behaviour. Unlike a street-shaped space, a square lends itself to meetings, whether arranged or by chance.

If the street-form is more suited to movement, the square-form is more likely to encourage lingering. You are under way in a street, whereas you arrive in a square.

The square suggests its spatial capacity for gatherings and encounters, even when there is nothing special going on there, thereby elevating it in importance above its surroundings. (This feeling comes unstuck when, inevitably it seems, it is used as a place to park.)

Squares arouse an element of centrality whereas streets, however important, are less likely to be foregrounded. If streets belong more to workaday life, squares generally are more useful for special occasions such as markets, celebrations and other gatherings.

In deliberately egalitarian plans, usually based on a grid, the aim is to decentralize the centre so that a multi-centrality ensues.[2] The intention then is to avoid a central square in the hope that as many streets as possible will take on a central duty.

Schools need both streets and squares. There has to be a square-like space where all pupils and teachers and often parents can gather for special events, but there must also be a street-like 'intersection' where all daily activities that are to be visible to everyone at all times are to be located.[3]

However varied the possible configurations for school plans, there will always be some kind of central square or an all-intersecting activity artery running through the building like a high street.

The larger the school, the more difficult it is to concentrate all central functions at one 'square'. So it is very difficult to avoid parts arising elsewhere where there is nothing to do; blind spots in the building where children feel shut out.

A main artery where all general amenities are concentrated, is therefore the only conceivable spatial means of retaining an overview of everything. This is the only way to prevent children from feeling lost in an excessively monolithic and chaotic-looking welter of parts all screaming for attention.

The more we articulate a space to everywhere attune it to intensive and varied use so as to enhance the small-scale aspect, the greater the need for a spatial theme running through it all to hold it together and, like a horizon to which all parts are related, unify it and make it easy to read.

2  See Free University, Berlin, pp. 160-162
3  The surface area is defining for the number of people able to
   occupy a space. Taking a given peripheral area into account, a
   city square has great advantages as it allows you to bring
   together relatively more people on a given surface area. So you
   are most likely to opt for a square shape and thus for the 'city
   square' form.

[1]

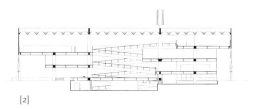

[2]

## Castelvittorio, Italy

If the tiny square at the centre of the little mountain settlement of Castelvittorio in Liguria seems to have been hewn out of the stone substance of tightly packed houses characterizing such communities, the little piazza is like the principal room of a fancifully formed residential building. Streets generally overhung with houses stab through this conglomeration to converge as if in a central hall. This is where the paths of the locals at their daily rounds cross. There are a few shops and cafés. The differences in height are expressed in the terraces along the frontage, side on to the piazza. They were probably put there on purpose, readily drawing on the uneven topography. These terraces become viewing balconies whenever there is something going on in the piazza, such as the annual tournament of 'pallone elastico', a variety of handball which the entire village turns out to watch,

[3]

[4]

lining the edge of the piazza in row upon row.

This is where daily life comes together. The urban space, which resembles a large living room in ambience and almost in size, adds to the community's social cohesion. Interestingly, the village church stands a short distance away with its own forecourt, so that its influence is not excessive.

This compact village, tacked onto a rock formation, can almost unequivocally be taken as a building. What must once have been a bare hilltop has been carved out to effectively circumscribe a village community with a social space at its heart.

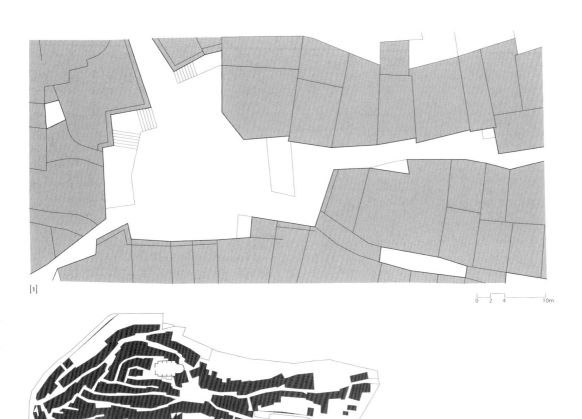

[1]

0  2  4      10m

[2]

[3]

[4] Titaan, Hoorn

## From assembly hall to square

It is not just the autonomy of the traditional classroom that has been put in perspective in the modern school paradigm; so has the assembly hall as the ceremonial space where the 'high points' of school life are cast into bold relief. An official assembly hall is not part of a school's daily life; it is only for holding special events for which it should be technically well-equipped to cater for musical and dramatic performances.

If such halls are customary in secondary schools and universities, they have always been a rare commodity in primary schools, at least in the Netherlands. In most cases, it is the gymnasium that performs this duty, with the easily scratched sports floor covered for the occasion.

If a school did have a hall specially made for assemblies, other general space had to suffer for it. Although every school in theory deserves such a facility, it is questionable whether it really justifies making what is usually a sealed-off space, given the reality of the limited means available.

The issue at hand is to find a form for a space where performances and productions, ceremonies and celebrations can take place in the totality of corridor and hall area, a form that makes sufficient room for such a demanding facility in what is a comparatively open situation. You have to see your way to making something that is just as appropriate for informal events, that is, all small-scale day-to-day situations, as for more formal ones.

Every school, then, needs a place to assemble for official or spontaneous gatherings, big enough to accommodate the entire school as well as the parents on occasion. The central space of the school on which everyone and everything converges will only be able to hold such numbers of people if you deploy every place that gives a view of what is happening. This means a maximum number of sight lines from galleries, stairs and treads which should double as seating, eliminating the need to endlessly drag chairs around whenever there is an event.

A central meeting space of this order has much of a city centre in miniature where there is always something to do. Here it is the space that makes the first move and thus encourages communal activity.

The older the pupils, in secondary school for instance, the greater their need for the opportunity to talk together, to hang around, use their phones, eat and drink. There are often vending machines, but a refreshment bar where you are served, expresses the fact that you are being taken seriously. This is absolutely the best way of inciting contact and encounter.

In fact, every school, primary schools too, should have a café as a central place where pupils, parents and teachers alike can unload or gather their thoughts.

The tradition that says that everybody has to go outside in the break is on the way out. Inside now has the quality of outside where table tennis, table football and videos provide more to do and to experience than out there on the paving stones round a desolate, isolated building.

## Secondary School, Agios Dimitrios, Athens, Greece, 1969-1974
Takis Zenetos, restored 2003-2005 by Y. Papaioannou, D. Papalexopoulus and K. Motsiou

After languishing for many years amidst rumours of demolition, the Agios Dimitrios school designed by Takis Zenetos has now been refurbished in its entirety and largely restored to its original form, including the auditorium below the central court.
The way the classrooms of this freestanding building enfold these two stacked courts recalls a city centre. It is a pity that upper court and lower court are unrelated spatially and function as two separate worlds, even though both represent indispensable aspects of a school community. Above, there is the open-air playground with the surrounding classrooms opening onto it and the galleries of the classrooms above overlooking it. This is where pupils come together informally. Below is a world wholly devoted to teaching and learning whose circular form fine-tunes the attention.

[1]

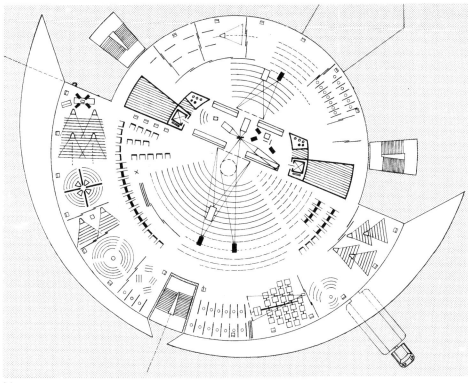

[2]

The original floor plan, an early example of a modern pedagogical model and a unique expression of a centre of learning, was left unrealized in the 1970s. Regrettably it proved equally impossible to achieve during the recent restoration, maybe through the current stance in Greek education. So it remains an example of a modern pedagogical model, although no longer Zenetos' original revelational couching of a communal ideal. It is not just the grouping of the classrooms and other rooms that organizes the space, but the structure as well. This is dominated by heavy concrete beams with unbelievably massive cantilevers typical of Zenetos. Duiker comes clearly to mind too, though at a distance, if only because of the explicit unifying presence of the structure.

[3]

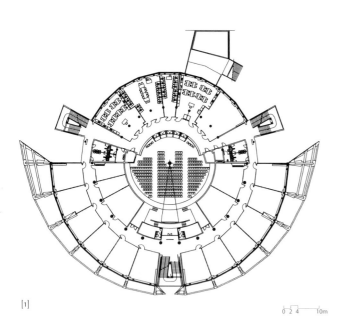

[1]

0  2  4    10m

[4]

[2]

[1] Reconstructed plan of lower floor

[2] Multipurpose hall after reconstruction

[3] Upper court

[4] Classroom gallery on first floor

[5] Hall space, De Eilanden Montessori primary school, Amsterdam

# Hall, De Eilanden Montessori Primary School, Amsterdam, 1996-2002

The hall space could only be realized at this size by including in it the playroom with its prescribed dimensions. This means that an entire wall is given over to equipment for physical exercises. The part allocated for this duty can be isolated with folding partitions.

These same partitions can also shape a stage area with the audience sitting in the sunken section. For more informal gatherings the stairs are the place to sit, supplemented by additional rows of compatible seating. Still more viewing opportunities are to be had from along the open balustrades on the upper storey which is joined

to the ground floor by a central well. The stair is also well-placed for sitting and watching. This hall is the undisputed centre of activity of the entire school and acts as a central square overlooked from the classrooms' prefatory spaces. Its elongated seat-steps demarcating the sunken part are where the most activity obtains at this transition between levels.

[1]

[2]

[3]

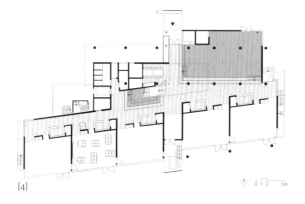

[4]

0 1 2    5m

[1, 2, 3] De Eilanden Montessori primary school, Amsterdam. A stage performance in the hall.

[4] Ground floor

[5] Video performance with audience in sunken area

## Hall, De Koperwiek Primary School, Venlo, 1995-1997

The sunken rectangle clearly defines itself as the focal point of the hall. Its unmistakable form is most likely the reason why children are less inclined to cross this place at will. This can be gauged from the respect shown to the fragile projects displayed there. After prolonged use, this place almost functions as a classroom without walls where certain rules seem to apply, comparable to the individual carpets in Montessori education but much larger and used more collectively.

[5]

[6]

The space is articulated as what is clearly a work area surrounded by circulation space. This configuration also holds out a form of spatial clarity that can keep together a group that would otherwise soon disperse throughout the hall. The adjoining play-room with opened partition can serve as a stage, with the 'hollow' squarely marking off the hall as the audience's domain.

[1]

[2]

[3]

[4]

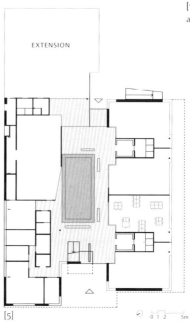

EXTENSION

[5]

[1, 2] Video performance with audience in sunken area

## Hall, Titaan, Hoorn, 2000-2004

The first in the sequence of stairs leading from the large central square up through the great well has been widened into tiers, resembling seating in a stadium, that turn the space into a theatre for performers or an auditorium for spectators. The folding doors of the music room open up to present a stage area.

On a school day, and particularly during breaks, the stairs, of which the first two turn the corner to give a U-shaped seemingly sunken space, are awash with pupils who

[6]

[7]

[8]

144  SPACE AND LEARNING

have come there to drink, chat, telephone, flirt and coax, provoke or just watch each other. Usually there are tables and chairs where you can sit together and where others can join you at will. Most prefer the more informal seating of the steps where you feel freer to come and go with no strings attached.

The U-shaped stairs encourage children to sit in a semicircle, expressing a sense of community, though with everyone retaining their freedom as individuals.

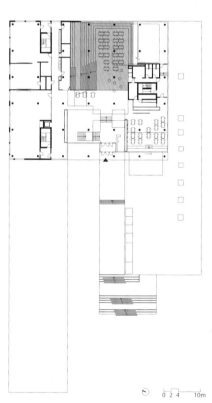

0 2 4    10m

[2] first floor

# Hall, Montessori College Oost, Amsterdam, 1993-1999

The hall of Montessori College Oost has to
be the most informal centre of any secondary school. It takes its cue from a stock of
mainly immigrant pupils who have little if
anything to fall back on as far as the Netherlands, Amsterdam and even their home life
are concerned. This and the tendency to be
isolated by their lack of language skills
meant that there was little point in including
theatre facilities. The large 'red square' sunk
several treads is diffuse in the way it extends
from a central core; it seems more evolved
than planned, much like the growth of old
town centres. All the central facilities are to
hand here including a general enquiry desk,
a post-school recruitment agency and a
refreshment bar. There is a direct access
from the hall to the workplaces and training
kitchens, and the void allows views up to
the classrooms.

[2]

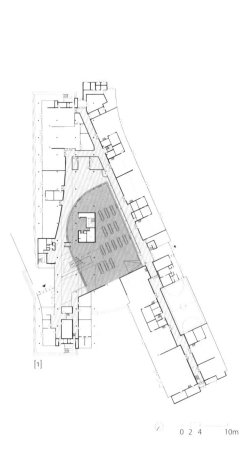

[1]

0 2 4    10m

[1]

[2]

[3]

[4]

Despite the absence of any clear suggestion of a theatre, this space proves remarkably easy to adapt to different uses, due to its versatility as well as its dimensions. Besides the awarding of certificates and festive occasions for the school itself, the space is regularly let for lectures and even concerts. The pupils seem to feel at home here; for them it is a house – and a city – where you can feel secure and have each other to fall back on.

The florid wall-hanging set against the rear of the central vertical core is a take on a wall painting in the old school, since demolished, by the 'Cobra' painter Anton Rooskens. The elemental force emanating from these pure forms and colours dominates the entire space. And though opinions of it must vary, no-one has ever laid a finger on it. After many years it is once again what it must have been, a glowing artefact radiating warmth and energy.

[5]

[6]

## Staffroom

No school is without a staffroom, a place where the teaching staff can withdraw to convene and write reports. With the increase in the number of teachers specialized in particular subjects, these rooms have simply been getting bigger and bigger. The staffroom is in fact the school's government centre, much like the municipal hall in the city, and the relationship between staff and pupils says much, if not everything, about relationships as a whole in the school. According to the conditions of employment in education, teachers have the right to a room that they can withdraw to, briefly escape from work, take a breather and vent their feelings on problem issues, which usually means difficult children. Still, during breaks they are expected to keep an eye on what is happening in the rest of the school and of course on the playground. So this room should have glazed walls or at least windows on all sides, so that there is little chance of anything happening unseen, however briefly.

The degree of openness of this staffroom expresses spatially the distance between teachers and pupils and the degree of hierarchy prevailing; the more open, the less evident that hierarchy. If pupils have access to the room and maybe are even allowed to work there, you see a situation of trust and community emerge. It expresses whether there is a regime or an atmosphere of teamwork. And that children could have access to what is said about them, as this could be lying around for all to see, is a minor risk when measured against the feeling pupils have of being treated equally and taken seriously.

[1]

[1]  Titaan, Hoorn

[2]  De Eilanden Montessori primary school, Amsterdam. Above: open staffroom where children may also work. Below: support point (the 'café') near the entrance.

[2]

## From library to study area

The library has traditionally been the most solemn space in a school building, if only because you always had to be mousey quiet there. It was where work was done, against a backdrop of books from where knowledge was to be drawn. It was the pre-eminent symbol of the intellectual presumption that a school sought to express. At other times it was little more than a reading nook where you might be able to borrow books.

A school library is before anything else a reading room where the emphasis is on study. So in principle it is a study area where peace and quiet prevails and everyone is individually immersed in what they are doing. There is scarcely anything of exchange, except eye contact perhaps. In principle, the conditions for concentration are nowhere better than here. In a reading room or study area concentration, even if feigned, is part of the social contract. It is simply not done to engage with others or attract their attention, let alone stand around chatting. Arguably, the reading and study area is the only part of the school to be accepted and respected as a more or less detached island, almost as a religious contemplation centre. That everyone there acts as an individual does nothing to alter the fact that a strong sense of community and even solidarity can prevail.

At one time the library was valued for preserving often priceless books and manu-

[1] Henri Labrouste, reading room of Bibliothèque Nationale, Paris, 1862-1868

[2, 3, 6, 7] Apollo schools, Amsterdam

[4] Louis Kahn, Philips Exeter Library, Exeter, New Hampshire, USA, 1968-1972

[5] Dominique Perrault, reading room of the Bibliothèque Nationale, Paris

[8] Hellerup Skole, Copenhagen, reading area

[6]

[1]

[2]

[3]

[4]

[5]

[7]

[8]

scripts, and so was a storehouse of intellectual and cultural values and a centre for accumulating knowledge. As this 'save, search and lend' duty lessened in importance, the emphasis came to lie on the character of a centre of learning, somewhat aloof perhaps from the world at large, a place where everything is everybody's and within reach and understanding. The accent now lies mainly on widening one's view of all those others immersed in their work and inciting one to do the same. But a centre of learning is also a prospect of all that preserved knowledge, more limited perhaps than the vast internet but more palpable. You don't need a library to look things up these days. In what used to be the library, the prime matter now is reading, listening, seeing, digesting, working. This way it is slowly reverting to what it once was, be it in another form; a space that incites study, the school's intellectual heart.

# Space for gymnastics and sports

Attempts to integrate gymnasiums and the generally much larger sports halls in school buildings are almost always doomed to failure. Because of their size they get housed in ill-fitting, lumpen volumes usually away from the main school.

The gymnasium has always been readily resorted to as a general assembly hall. The need for gymnasiums is undiminished and is expected to increase as local amenities become integrated. We need only think of the festivals and religious meetings of the many ethnic groups who have no suitable premises of their own.

Modernist ideas turned physical education into a serious school subject that made steadily greater demands on the gymnasium space. The floor with its restrictions on footwear, an even spread of light (meaning artificial lighting), the ever more technocratically tinged rules and regulations informing changing and washing rooms and other secondary facilities – all these served to increasingly separate such spaces from the rest of the school both physically and psychologically. This has undoubtedly been helped along by the exploitational motive of letting the premises to local sports associations who have their own ever more stringent requirements. The emphasis has increasingly come to lie on achieving, in other words on difficult and for real rather than exciting and for fun. Still, it is impossible to overestimate the importance of sports and games as a part of school life. To effectively integrate these activities spatially is certain to have a positive effect on the air of activity at school. Doing gymnastics as a regular part of the school day and watching sports, exercise and games, frees up energy and is inspirational, galvanizing and motivating, no doubt also for those who spend most of their traditional education sitting still. And having an audience gets better performances out of the players.

[1, 2, 5] De Polygoon primary school, Almere

[3, 4] Günther Behnisch, St. Benno Gymnasium, Dresden, 1996

[6] Hellerup Skole, Gentofte, Copenhagen, 2002

[1]

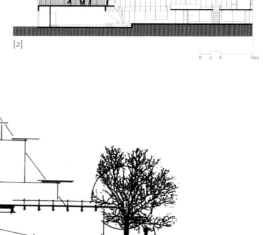

[2]

0 2 4 10m

[3]

[4]

[5]

[6]

So it makes sense to insist that sports facilities should be visually linked to the school, integrated instead of being parked in boxes away from it.

If school is a place to practice social behaviour, then sports and games have a key duty to perform there, such as developing a healthy competitive attitude and measuring yourself against others within clear rules. Children gain respect and self-confidence from their sporting achievements, certainly when the space is such that they can be observed and taken note of by others.

[1]

[2]

[3]

[4]

## Hans Scharoun

One architect who applied himself to space for learning with dedication and conviction was Hans Scharoun. Of the four schools he designed between 1951 and 1966 two were built, of which the Geschwister Scholl School (1956-1962) in Lünen, Westphalia, most fully expresses his ideas.

Scharoun was the first architect to attempt to translate into spatial terms his ideas, clearly derived from the anthroposophical teachings of Rudolf Steiner, about the school not just as an institute but as an environment where learning was not restricted to regular education and geared instead to shaping the entire personality and preparing the individual for their entry into society and for the responsibilities they are to take there. Scharoun's objective, then, was char-acter-building and creating an awareness that would enable the individual to take part in a qualitatively responsible way and contribute to public life and the political foundations in which it is rooted.

"The most important task of education is the insertion of the individual into the community through the development of a sense of personal responsibility, in such a way that the community that results represents more than the sum total of individuals it contains. This aspect of education cannot be taught directly, it is rather a matter of general experience and the gradual forma-tion of consciousness which allows the individual to find the right contact with public life and with the political community."[4]

This all seems rather high-flown and it is questionable whether Scharoun did in fact manage to render this spatially, yet his ideas, also those inspired by Steiner, are certainly remarkable and still relevant today. At all events, these notions proceeding from the makeability of a harmonious society are light years away from the society we live in today. Still, at least there are those who consider and attempt worthwhile solutions to the existing simplified situation of rows of rectangular classrooms off corridors. This gives Scharoun the honour of being the first to characterize school as a micro-urban society. For the record, the theatre space was invariably at the building's centre. His contextual preoccupation led each time to fairly fragmented buildings, more landscape than built structure, with classrooms

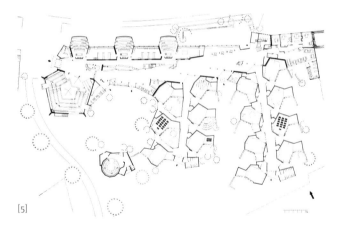

[5]

[1]  Galli & Rudolf Architects, Zurich
International School, Zurich,
Switzerland, 1999-2002

[2]  Architectenbureau Marlies
Rohmer, Terwesten primary school,
The Hague, 2001-2005

[3]  Fire station, Zwolle,
Architectuurstudio HH
[4]  School, London

[5, 6]  Geschwister Scholl School,
Lünen, Westphalia, Germany,
1956-1962

[6]

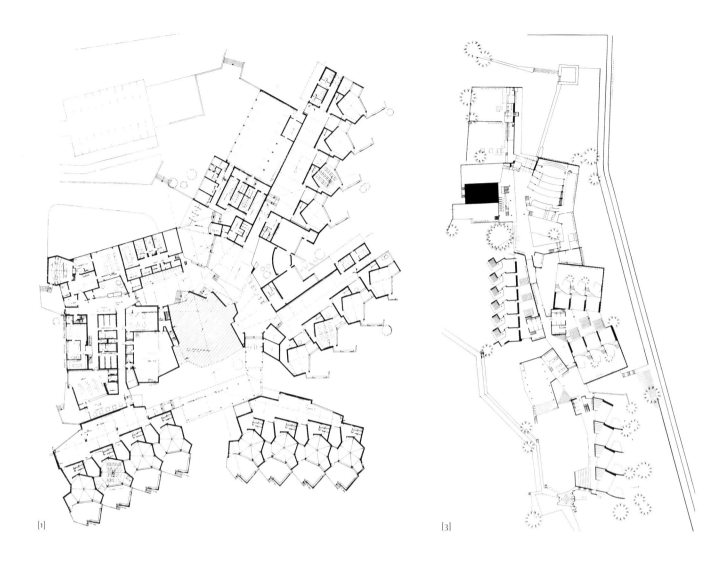

[1]

[3]

[2]

[1, 2] Haupt- und Grundschule, Marl, Westphalia, Germany, 1957-1958

[3] Volksschule, Darmstadt, Germany, 1951

[4-6] Peter Hübner, Evangelische Gesamtschule, Gelsenkirchen, Germany, 2004

expressed inwards and to the surroundings as discrete 'houses'. This accords with his postulation that from a pedagogical point of view every classroom should be a *Schulwohnung* or school-house. In spite of the open-looking floor plans, assembled from many components whose constant shifts of alignment suggest handwriting, his designs seem unable to avoid the same sense of hermetic thinking characterizing the 'free' style of anthroposophical architecture with its often laboured avoidance of right angles. The fear of a clear, easy-to-read structure, in our opinion germane to all good architecture and urbanism, prevails on all fronts. His organic, or rather landscape-related handwriting led him to fine, free spatial configurations which, alas, he failed to convert into an effective architecture and which each time remained caught in fragmentary conglomerates of fairly banal parts.

And yet Scharoun worked along principled and to some extent consistent lines. His open floor plans of an almost nest-like structure at no time suggest that they had grown over time, as is all too often the case with the younger generation of mainly German architects he influenced. To make a school literally like an old town – in other words as if people once lived round a village square where there are now classrooms – is admittedly enticing in the decorative sense and perhaps works well as a school. Given its nostalgic undertone, however, it does little to further the quest for forms for the modern school, a quest Scharoun was undeniably engaged on.

4 Hans Scharoun, 'Raum und Milieu der Schule', Vortrag auf der XI. Triennale Bauen + Wohnen, Bauen + Wohnen, 16. Jg., München 1962, Nr. 4, S. IV/4. Text of the lecture given by Scharoun in 1962 at the Eleventh Triennale 'Bauen + Wohnen', as quoted in translation in both monographs on the architect by Peter Blundell-Jones (Gordon Fraser 1978 and Phaidon 1995).

[4]

[5]

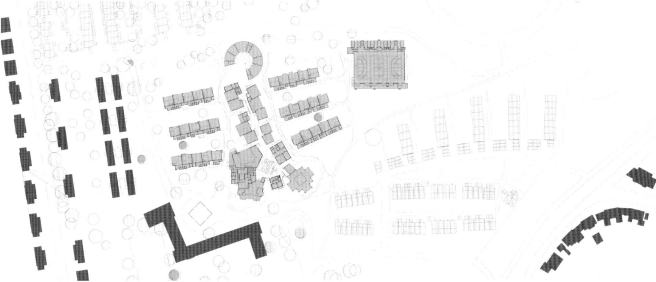

[6]

## Free University, Berlin, 1963
## Candilis, Josic and Woods

Shadrach Woods' design of 1963 for the Berlin Free University was without question the first building for education to be organized like a city and the outcome of an ideological thought process.[5] Woods, like his friend and colleague Giancarlo de Carlo, propagated not just the idea of the 'educational city' with its emphasis on the Marxist notion of emancipation, but sought a contextual model for a large institute of education that might accommodate the intrinsic uncertainty resulting from the rapid changes that even then were unsteadying the world, and certainly the university, by means of a far-reaching disposition for accepting change. He went so far in this as to stipulate that parts of the building had to be demountable and thus able to be moved around or replaced. Aside from the technical issues, this could be done using a system of unchangeable main connecting corridors, like main streets through the building. This network of main streets constituted the building's structure off which the different institutes with their teaching/learning spaces and offices could be 'slung' and 'unslung' at will.

Regrettably, this revolutionary promise fails to shine through in the project as built. Not only did nothing come of the disassembly aspect (something that would certainly have been possible with the excruciatingly bare prefab school rooms of our own time), but the network of main streets through the building in fact became a common-or-garden system of corridors. This dealt

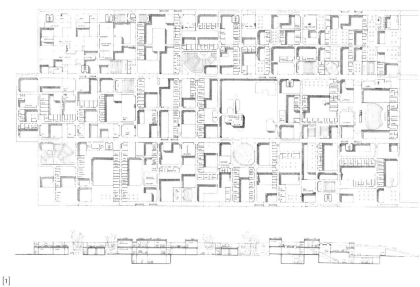

[1]

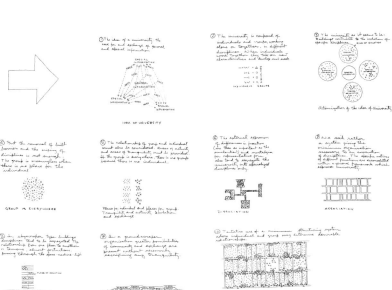

[2]

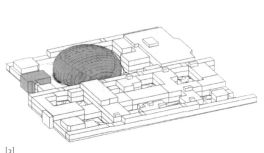

[3]

[4]

[1] Design for the Berlin Free University

[2] Explanation of the design

[3] Diagram from 2005 with Norman Foster's new library

[4] Passage Galerie Vivienne, Paris, 1823-1826

[5, 6] Berlin Free University in 2007

[7] Free University in 2007 with entrance to new library

[5]

[6]

[7]

the death blow to what had been a brilliant idea. The building became a maze of passages like so many other run-of-the-mill buildings.

To turn a corridor into a street, apart from using materials that evoke associations with outside, requires greater dimensions and more than anything else a greater height, preferably toplit with natural light as in the 19th-century arcades in Paris. Again, the 'streets' of the Berlin university have no workplaces along them or other elements that incite use and contact with others. The point is that if you should meet anyone you can stop and talk for a longer or shorter time, providing of course that that space occasions you to do so.

So in the end it was architectural excess that prevented this highly impressive idea from bearing fruit. Later enlargements, by Henning Larsen in 1973-1981 and Norman Foster in 1997-2005, made no attempt to infuse the concept with new life and thus save it – quite the reverse in fact. Particularly Norman Foster's out-of-place dome, dominating the proceedings in what had begun as such an egalitarian scheme, was the kiss of death for Shadrach Woods' brilliant idea, which these days is scarcely discernible in the project, not least thanks to a thorough sprucing-up.

Leaving aside what has happened to it in practice, this project may well be the very first true structuralist concept; an unchanging, extendable structure that can accept and enable local changes in infill.

The idea of structuralism was derived from linguistic theory, where it proceeded from the dichotomy of language and speech.[6] In 1957 Noam Chomsky in his book *Syntactic Structures* used the concepts of 'competence' and 'performance' to indicate a distinction between what in principle is a guiding and immutable structure and the variable and varied infill which, compared with the structure, operates to a short time cycle. In urban design terms you might compare this principle to a street that stands the test of time while each of the buildings that constitute it is exposed to change in occupancy and, inevitably, in appearance.

A characteristic of structuralism is the dialectic of change and remaining itself. We are talking about a 'system' that opens up to change and is able to accept this change without actually changing itself. So structuralism in its authentic guise opens up all perspectives for a building to be able to hold its ground and at the same time attune itself to the programmatic uncertainty that holds sway over all our designs from start to finish. Essential to structuralism is the openness of the system, a fundamental incompleteness, more like a city that keeps changing than a well-rounded architectural composition, which is how architects like to see their buildings. Few architects have used structuralism in such a radical sense as Shadrach Woods.

There are many buildings which are unable to accept change, although their outward appearance suggests otherwise, as the architect did not explicitly proceed from this particular quality. Generally speaking, the fact that a building transforms over time, and thus is exposed to the whims of its users, is not the first thought to enter its architect's head. Le Corbusier's design for a hospital in Venice and Aldo van Eyck's Orphanage in Amsterdam are often singled out as the first structuralist buildings. But though at first sight they seem capable of accepting any amount of change, they are in fact utterly inviolable both inside and outside. We cannot say this for sure about that of Le Corbusier, as regrettably it was never built. But in Van Eyck's case there can be no doubt that he sought to keep his buildings in the exact state in which they were designed.[7] Although the Orphanage, as 'both palace and settlement', is peerless in its capacity to accept changes of occupancy, this was clearly not what Van Eyck had in mind.[8] In fact he designed the interior, such as the original built furniture, with equal devotion and as one with the building's 'structure'. For him there was no such thing as a distinction between structure and infill. Van Eyck was certainly no structuralist in the way Shadrach Woods was, but it is just as certain that Aldo van Eyck was the better architect.

5 See *Lessons for Students in Architecture*, pp. 116, 117
6 Ferdinand de Saussure (1857-1913) made a distinction between *la langue* and *la parole* in the lectures he gave at the University of Geneva between 1906 and 1911.
7 A conflict broke out even as construction was under way, about modifications required of the architect in view of the recently changed ideas on education, modifications which according to Van Eyck could no longer be implemented in the building. Later when the Berlage Institute, a school for architects no less, appropriated much of the building, Van Eyck had the greatest difficulty with even the tiniest changes made to it. As it happens, the Orphanage proved eminently suited to its new educational duty.
8 See *Space and the Architect: Lessons 2*, pp. 198, 199

[1] Le Corbusier, design for a hospital in Venice, Italy, 1964-1965

[2] Aldo van Eyck, plan of Orphanage, Amsterdam, 1959-1961

[3] Spruced-up exterior of Berlin Free University

[4] Entrance to library (Norman Foster)

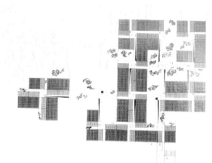

[1]

[2]

[3]

[4]

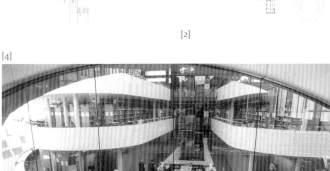

## Pedregulho Complex, Rio de Janeiro, Brazil, 1950-1952
## Affonso Eduardo Reidy

What is exceptional about the Pedregulho complex is its combination of a school and housing in an ensemble that radiates innovation and hope. If modern architecture has anywhere become the countenance of a better future, it is here. Particularly Europeans found it difficult to grasp that although these elegant, freestanding and fanciful lightweight forms were visually tied together, they were in no way part of a larger, urban entity. Now, more than fifty years on, these seemingly free forms engage as if naturally with their surroundings which hem them in on all sides. Meanwhile, the ribbon of housing snaking across the mountain slope has since shown all the signs of social dilapidation and the infills within what are still the sharply defined lines of its floors have become almost favela-like. Remarkably, the school is still entirely intact and has stayed up to date. It is hard to believe, then, that the children swimming in the limpid swimming pool below are the same children living in the hovels above.

Still the school, its distinctive forms dominated by colourful compositions in glazed tiles, spills out its optimistic narrative, one linked with this architecture from day one. Not that the school has anything to show in

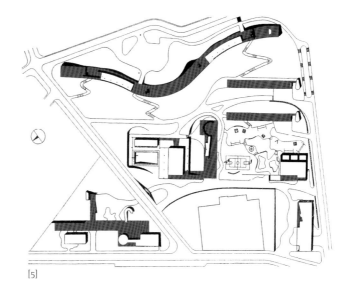

[5]

[6]

[7]

the way of innovative ideas on education; off its long fairly narrow corridor are regular classrooms, although these do boast full-width balconies at least 3.5 metres deep for working outside.

What is most striking about Brazilian modern architecture is its lack of a 'skin', let alone a barrier between inside and outside. Buildings are not surrounded and defined by an outer skin as they are here for the necessary climatological separation. There, inside and outside are one and the same spatial entity, giving a great sense of freedom and with a loose-fit feel that allows everything to breathe. Instead of the paucity of our well-off regions where everything is measured off to the nearest centimetre, this architecture is generous and accommodating, showing us in spatial terms how education can mean a better future for society.

[3]

[4]

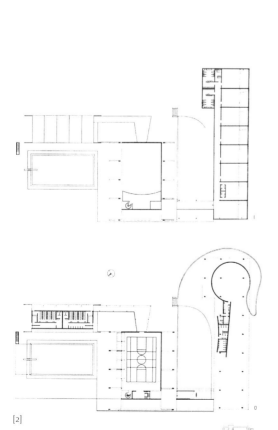

[2]

[5]

[1]

## Schools in Nagele, 1954-1956
## Aldo van Eyck and H.P.D. van Ginkel

The three schools commissioned from Aldo van Eyck for the brand-new village of Nagele designed by the Dutch wing of CIAM (Congrès Internationale d'Architecture Moderne) in the Noordoostpolder (North East Polder) which had been drained in 1942, are an early example of a composition of classrooms shifted relative to one another to enfold a central space resembling a town square.

"By simply staggering the classrooms in two groups of three instead of designing the usual straight row, two important things happen: the resulting exterior classroom corners provide a wider view whilst the interior corners now become tall in-between spaces which penetrate the classrooms articulating them so they can be used for any activity that may take place between them; an interior for the school as a social community also. Here, a single gesture has simultaneously opened up the view to the outside and to the inside, the one the result of the other.

"Outwards, held within the large concrete window frames, a wider view of the surroundings gives one a greater feeling of belonging. Inside, brought into focus by the entrance areas greater visual contact is made possible: a primary condition for greater involvement."[9]

The principle of shifting the classrooms produces an open corner, giving each classroom a bay window-like view out and a porch-like entrance. This last-named is also the reason for a square corridor section, belonging as it were to one and two classrooms respectively. Instead of a simple corridor along the classrooms what we see here is an articulation assembled from corridor elements whose shifting in and out of alignment gives a a suggestion of places, unlike a circulation corridor.

Even here the classrooms are autonomous and sealed off from one another and from the hall, but together they shape the hall as a complementary space which in principle can also be used for education. Further, the outdoor playground is also drawn into the narrative by the additional entrance porches. All in all, this school design, based as it is on numbers and shifted figures, opens in formal terms the door to equality of all parts and their use for activities, as has since become customary in today's concept of education.

These schools in Nagele, more than any other single building, were a model for the Montessori School in Delft (see pp. 31, 115, 116), although this last-named is looser in its composition, which enabled the later enlargements and thus a change in the original layout. You might regard the Delft Montessori School as a practical actualization of the equal and complementary use of the corridor space touted in Nagele, at least in the formal sense, which can therefore be seen as the first step in the evolution from corridor to school hall.

9  Herman Hertzberger, 'The mechanism of the twentieth century and the architecture of Aldo van Eyck', in *Aldo van Eyck*, Amsterdam: Stichting Wonen, 1982, p. 10

[1]

[2]

[3]

[4]

[5]

[3] Entry porch in 2007

[2, 4, 5] Photos from 1956

# The Extended School, a sociocultural complex

The last stage in the process of eliminating the traditional school building is to integrate it in a sociocultural complex, what we in the Netherlands call a Brede School, an 'Extended School' or 'Community School'.

This new conglomeration assembles together the schools in a neighbourhood or city area – in the Netherlands this means schools of different 'blood groups' such as Protestant, Catholic, government-run or Muslim – with before and after school support and other community welfare facilities. It is also an inducement for adding to it other local amenities including a library, sports halls, a school of music, a social and medical aid centre and a community centre. Incorporating sports facilities and the local library is particularly attractive to children and for the library a reason to take a deliberately educational line.

With the tendency to choose a school on grounds of faith gradually disappearing, many schools threaten to become marginalized and the government is confronted with closure on the one hand and the need for more school space on the other, when it is anybody's guess what the future make-up of the school population will be. The so-called Extended School offers a way out by bringing several schools together in one place for reasons of 'flexibility', social cohesion and of course to keep costs down. There are also financial advantages to be had from combining schools and sharing accommodation; the average budget for a school in the Netherlands is not enough to include the construction of your own assembly hall space.

[2]

You might object to such developments if you were only to look at the motives of the tight-fisted authorities for cutting back on social and cultural budgets. Even so, the Extended School can result in unquestionably useful sociospatial models. There is also a practical advantage for parents bringing and collecting their children, that everything is in one place.

[1]

The greatest concern among schools that find themselves having to coexist is that of losing what they term their own identity, and its expression in the building. The architect is expected to cleverly patch this up and this way smooth the ruffled feathers. But identity is not something that can be made to measure or applied like a coat of paint. A school's identity, for example, derives from the common body of ideas accumulated by a particular group over time, one which all concerned can identify with.

A more serious consideration is that architects should take the raft of interests expressed in an extreme form of compartmentalization and weld them into a manage-

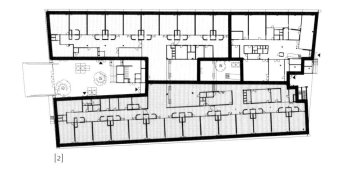

[2]

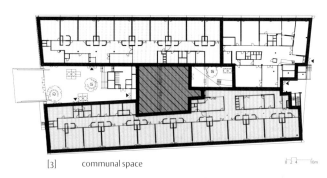

[3]    communal space

0  2  4      10m

[4]

[5]

[6]

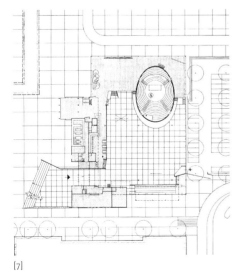

[7]

[1-4] Meerwijk Extended School, Haarlem

[5-7] Frank van Klingeren, De Meerpaal, Dronten, 1965-1967 (photo 6 by Jan Versnel)

able and easy-to-read whole that each of the institutions can recognize themselves in and that gives spatial expression to the obvious advantages and greater potential of shared use, as against thinking exclusively in terms of territories.

What matters most is that the institutions in the complex must remain independent components so as to be able to retain their identity. On the other hand, they should not be kept separate to the extent that, though sharing a building and perhaps the main entrance, they are in fact discrete entities like apartments in a block of flats where the only contact is the indirect one between those who mess up the entrance hall and those who clean up afterwards. An entirely open configuration, where you are condemned to each other's company, is not the answer either. This is why the community centres propagated and designed in 1966 and 1967 by Frank van Klingeren, while famous as concepts, in practice failed to meet the claims made of them.[10] Whenever openness is elevated to a credo without due thought being given to fitness of purpose, inconvenience and misuse will prevail over good intentions. It should be said that these concentrations of activities under a single large roof were predicated more on the social Utopia everyone was full of in those days than on intelligently responding to social reality. One of these centres, De Meerpaal in Dronten, was recently refurbished from top to bottom, leaving little of the original openness.

In short, it is all about striking the right balance between individuality and community, a balance expressed in the way the space is divided and organized and founded on what those using it want to be able to do alone and as a group, in other words which spaces are to be shared and which are not.

Just as single schools went through the process from traditional classrooms to more open situations with the learning landscape the most extreme form, Extended Schools need to find forms of spatial connectedness between the constituent schools that weld it all together. The underlying premise here is that while each school must remain its own spatial unit, the spatial organization must incite contact and joint activities. It goes without saying that in combining schools with other facilities for children you can afford to have much bigger and better equipped communal spaces, certainly when there are also local services on board. It is of course still so that rooms for music, drama, visual expression and handiwork are the exception rather than the rule. And so cultural training remains the preserve of those few children whose parents have become aware of its importance and can afford an expensive private facility.

In the common centre of the Extended School, each of the coexisting schools and institutions can organize its own activities in consultation with the others. Then each individual unit becomes acquainted with what the others are doing, so that along with the fuss comes understanding and an idea of when to back off and make space for others. It can also lead to all these different worlds mixing and each gaining in magnitude as a result. A most important point is to articulate the space in such a way that smaller groups find a place in it without feeling lost in too large an expanse.

Whenever the various schools and other institutions coexisting in an Extended School actually start working together and get to the stage of jointly organizing major events, if you add up all the children and all the teachers it gives you a very large group that can easily compare with the population of a prevocational secondary school. It fills the space they share to the brim. This can create an atmosphere of togetherness necessary for the success of an Extended School.

You must be able to make use of each other's facilities and so profit from what others are good at. One school has a strong leaning towards music, the other towards drama, so they have something to offer each other; at least they have if the architect takes care of the spatial preconditions, such as being able to enter each other's school easily and that the correct visual accessibility obtains.

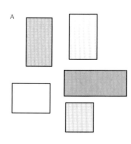

During the design process, the architect has to contend with discord and mistrust between one school and another. This is understandable when you have to forfeit your autonomy for the common interest, unknown and uncontrollable as this is. (There have been cases of mutant lizards born with two heads that squabble over a prey that will end up in one and the same stomach.) It is no easy job making the different parties aware of the advantages of the enterprise they have engaged in, or were forced to engage in by the authorities to qualify for financial support in getting new premises built. Whether this new form of school building project is a favourable development largely depends on whether teachers at different schools can work together so as to enjoy the advantages of a wider choice. In this they are more dependent than ever on the spatial possibilities given them by the architect. The most important aspect, then, is to show that combining forces is advantageous to all concerned. This new spatial potential and the considerable enrichment it brings to the programme finds us a step closer to the notion of the school as a city.

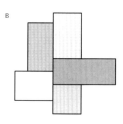

Once the plans for an Extended School are under way, it becomes an attractive proposition for many, often fringe institutions at the neighbourhood level. This gives us a building type that should not just be capable of coping with the greatest internal upheavals but also be receptive to any number of changes in programme and, of course, able to be added to externally.

When schools and local amenities join forces, the obvious place for them is at the centre of the neighbourhood or city, thus moving the school away from its position on the outskirts.

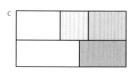

The combining of community welfare services and cultural institutions into a multi-functional complex is a new idea that holds out attractive advantages for facilities that individually are often too weak to keep their heads above water and find premises of their own. In this set-up, the schools are the body to which the other members attach themselves. Together they can become a force to be reckoned with and perhaps even see their way to countering the monoculture of the commercial centres which are forcing themselves on residential estates with increasing arrogance. It also releases the schools from their banishment to the open green outskirts and brings them back into the centre of neighbourhoods and districts.

This gives rise to the perspective of the learning environment, not as an autonomous, exclusive institute like the monumental school buildings of former times, but integrated into the bigger picture of social facilities.

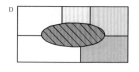

The emergence of sociocultural complexes signals the end of the self-sufficient school building. Their hook-up with other so-called service providers will usher in a new hybrid building type closer to a larger species of community centre than a school. For the schools themselves, the blurring of their borders and therefore their territory is a spur to collaboration.

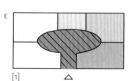

[1]

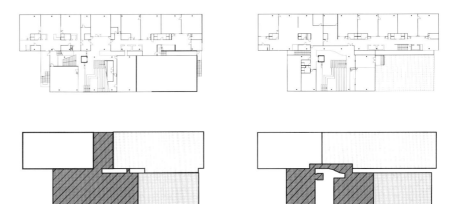

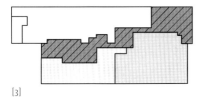

[2]

[3]

communal space

[1] Ingredients (A) are organized
into an Extended School (B) and
then given architectural unity (C) in
such a way as to permit a space for
common use (D). With all components accessed primarily from the
communal space, this takes on the
ambience of a central square (E).

[2] De Spil Extended School,
Arnhem

As for the children, they will find themselves in an environment where there is more
to experience and assimilate that in a school building. Learning is then a more inclusive, more natural part of community life and of the city.

For the architect, this development goes further than simply adding briefs together,
and signifies a new challenge. The pioneering role played by schools in multifunctional complexes places the emphasis here on education and learning and therefore
on a new substance, one perhaps more concrete than the non-committal element of
encounter colouring community centres in the past.

10  See *Lessons for Students in Architecture*, p. 70

[1]

# The school entrance

This is where children wait for each other and parents bring and collect the younger ones. A pre-eminent social hub for all age groups, it is where children arrange to go to each other's homes, and where parents meet.

It is a threshold, an area where school and the public realm overlap. It should at least include somewhere to sit, however informal, while some form of shelter from the weather is always welcome. But as long as the fear of attracting undesirable young loafers persists, it will continue to raise objections from the school that might just subside if the entire public domain essentially were to become less desolate and more hospitable.

Extended Schools, or Community Schools, consist of a number of autonomous units each with its own entrance, if only because they operate as independent institutions. It is sensible to turn these entrances as much as possible towards each other and have them lead into a shared interior zone where everything common to them can be expressed, and that behaves like a square or street, strengthening and giving substance to the feeling of cityness.

So what matters is how this city-like conglomeration is to be made accessible. The less Extended Schools are regarded as freestanding buildings and are increasingly assimilated in the urban fabric, the more logical the idea of informal entrances. As more

[2]

community-oriented and other more general functions become part of it, the building's interior will gain a stronger public and consequently more urban aspect. Then the schools and the other institutions will figure as distinct, maybe even maverick elements, each with its own pronounced entrance, rather like shops in a mall.

[3]

[1]

[2]

[1, 2] Apollo schools, Amsterdam

[3-5] De Eilanden Montessori primary school, Amsterdam

[4]

[5]

# The schoolyard

The traditional school playground or schoolyard is a large paved surface in front of the building, or behind it whenever this was necessary to slot the school into a regular city block. You enter it directly from the street and so there is no fence between street and

playground. Children are able to run in the playground and that really is about all, unless there is a climbing frame, in which case they climb as well. It is hard not to associate the sight of children in an enclosed compound with prisoners in an exercise yard, so this act of screening them from the surroundings is manifest and unequivocal. There are parallels to be drawn between the traditional playground and the autono-

[2]

[1]

[2]

mous classroom. Both act as closed systems, with no trade-off with their immediate surroundings and so express a kind of autism that the outside world experiences as threat-
ening or at least disturbing. By regarding the environment as hostile or the school as
hostile to its environment, the school becomes a prison with no communication between it and the world outside.

So the traditional school playground gets little further than a facility for getting rid of
pent-up energy and this 'concept' belongs in all respects to a learning situation where
children have to sit still when in class, and when outside are merely kept busy running
about without learning much in the process. Seen this way, playground and classroom
are the same old archetype outside and inside: for the children it is literally all or nothing, running about or sitting still. The often present playground equipment on which
you can hone your skills makes up for it to some extent, but is a little one-sided in
terms of physical activity.

Playgrounds should be attuned to practising social behaviour, and architects should be
thinking about how to create the spatial conditions that might encourage this
approach.

## Walls, Montessori School, Delft, 1960-1966

The low parallel walls that gave the territory behind the school its distinctive structure have since disappeared. When they proved to have subsided in places after some thirty years' duty, they were demolished and replaced by a field of concrete tiles with a few sad items of standard play equipment, after deliberation with the parents but without consulting the architect. The edges of the concrete blocks were probably considered unsafe on the strength of the occasional grazed knee. Ever more intrusive security standards are slowly killing off everything that rises above the unbearable deferential mean and so children are kept away from every danger, let alone given a taste for it.

The original network of walls was made as a framework for sandpits and little gardens and encouraged all kinds of additions by the children themselves. This meant that they

[3]

[4]

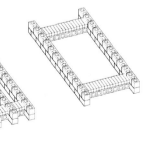

[5]

could be transformed from place to place into the forms and changes of meaning given them in the associations made by the children. Thus, for instance, at times and in places they were the beginnings of a tent and the sandpits became houses and shops.[11] They may have been simple walls, but partly due to the highly intriguing perforated

blocks that comprised them they together became a set of tools that the children could use and thus an invitation to a world of personal and shared interpretations. In other words they fired the imagination, something you cannot say about the unattractive, facile paving that has replaced them.

11 See *Lessons for Students in Architecture*, pp. 154, 155, 168, 169

[2]

[3]

[4]

## Gully, Montessori School, Delft, 1960-1966

The network of low walls was traversed by a water-filled gully, together with the sand a source of discoveries and experiences, where inevitably, as with every water course through an inhabited area, a healthy dose of social skills was called into play.
The obvious educational possibilities of water and sand were clearly too much for the teaching staff. They also had to explain to parents why their children were coming home covered in mud.

[1]

## Between street and playground, Montessori School, Delft, 1960-1966

The only thing separating the school's public forecourt from the street is a low brick walk, now solid but originally assembled from blocks with square openings (intended for ventilation) where your foot could fit or a rope could be tied for skipping. Despite its mass it expressed a degree of transparency. This low perforated wall articulates the school forecourt, although it is part of the public street space with a regular pavement. For the children it is a threshold between street zone and school zone, a place to linger where there is a degree of shelter; for the footballers among them, it marks out an area where they can emulate their heroes pretty well undisturbed by those living round about.

[2]

## Sandpits and gardens, Apollo Schools, Amsterdam, 1981-1983

As a variation on the now demolished sand-pits of the Montessori School in Delft, the sandpits at the Apollo Schools are arranged in two rows with the same dimensions as those in Delft. They lie along an elongated larger sandpit, laid out as if a small street with houses on either side, in a form familiar to us from archaeological excavations. As we have seen in Delft, the squares are indeed interpreted by small groups of children as little houses, while the elongated sand-street incites a more collective use.
A reorganization has meant that the toddlers have been rehoused in another build-ing, so that this miniature city can no longer be used as a sandpit. It has since been transformed into little gardens, though without any cause to modify the structure; this remains valid as long as it's a question of grouping 'private' units off a 'collective' zone.
This elongated communal area has since been paved with a surprising variety of tiles. The upshot is a garden path such as one you might conceivably come across somewhere in an exotic garden; its former duty as a sandpit is erased from the memory.

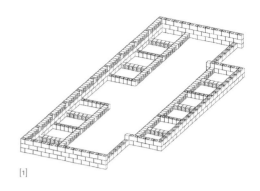

[1]

[2]

[3]

[4]

[5]

[6]

[7]

## Outdoor classes, Apollo Schools, Amsterdam, 1981-1983

The grounds of the Apollo Schools are shared by three schools. There is no question of a front and a rear, not least because the buildings have been bedded into site as detached objects. The space has however been articulated into a number of zones divided up by lots of little walls. These walls form corners that lend themselves to giving lessons to groups of children. Here too the concrete blocks have square ventilation holes in them, so that they are not only more or less transparent but also, as it were, permeable for use.

[1]

[2]

[3]

[4]

[5]

# Outside stair, De Evenaar Primary School, Amsterdam, 1984-1986

The broad stair leading to the entrance to De Evenaar primary school in Amsterdam-Oost is not just to make the school readily accessible but also acts as seating for the public playground, where the neighbourhood makes as great a claim on it as the school. The school building, sited on a local square surrounded on three sides by housing, only had one small fenced-off play space raised several treads on the south side for the youngest children. Otherwise there are no fences and the play area is shared by the neighbourhood.

When the local public space was reorganized recently, the toddlers' play space disappeared to be replaced by an all-engulfing public play area with elaborate play and sports apparatus overrunning the entire square and leaving scarcely any room to play football, thereby robbing the seat-steps of their broader duty.

[1]

[2]

[3]

## Sitting-wall, Montessori College Oost, Amsterdam, 1993-1999

This low wall, set parallel along the entire length of the front facade and interrupted only by the main entrance to the school, defines the width of the public pavement and the strip alongside it. Everything between the wall and the facade is school territory. Before and after school hours, the children hang around rather than play, coaxing and provoking dates the way boys and girls that age do. And this requires places that allow and incite such behaviour. On the front and back of this sitting-wall are some 1200 mosaic tiles, each made by a pupil under the supervision of Akelei Hertzberger, whose idea was to incorporate a poem that would appeal to the children by Dutch actor-poet-singer Huub van der Lubbe, with a letter worked into each tile. So the tiles literally had a prescribed part with a common meaning and a free part where everyone could express their own ideas, limited though it was to a single tile. This wall is thus a 'message' from the school to the public realm, but most of all it got the pupils at that time to engage with the building and its construction.

[4]

[5] (photo Maurice Boyer)

## Shelter, De Polygoon Primary School, Almere, 1991-1992

This free-standing basic facility consists of a concrete slab as a plinth to sit on and a steel lean-to roof. Protecting against rain and sun, it is an anchor and a given when playing outside but also a place to sit and an awning for waiting beyond the school entrance. It is an alternative for a facility, usually attached to the building, that never gets accepted out of fear that it will attract the wrong element.

[1]

[2]

## Playground, De Vogels Primary School, Oegstgeest, 1998-2000

With houses and a school crammed together on this excessively small site, the possibilities of playing outside for both the school and the neighbourhood looked slender. By lifting up the school, however, we could create additional street space with its own roof too. The smallest children have their own rooftop play terrace feeding directly into their part of the school with a view out across the neighbouring houses. Down below, the outdoor stair accessing the school begins as a tier of seating overlooking the sunken part several treads deep. This part, besides, is screened off from the nearby houses by walls so that youngsters can play football there without disturbing the residents unduly.

[3]

[4]

[5]

# Timeline, Anne Frank Primary School, Papendrecht, 1993-1994

In what was originally an idea by Akelei Hertzberger, children in their last year at this school in Papendrecht fill in the hole in a concrete tile with a mosaic, adding their personal testimony to the playground.

This way each pupil literally leaves their mark behind as a memento.

The personal infills are, as it were, held in a receiving framework of black and white tiles along with other tiles containing details of bicycles and distinguishing marks as used on cycle paths and in car parks, elements the concrete trade was able to dispense with. Year by year, the resulting ribbon gradually edges its way round the school.

[1]

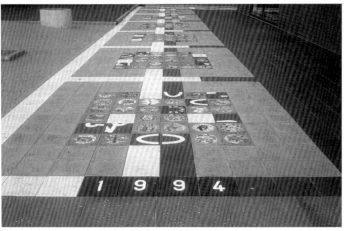

[2]

[3]

## Playground, De Eilanden Montessori Primary School, Amsterdam, 1996-2002

This school has no grounds of its own save for a strip less than two metres wide along the classroom side, bordering on the car park of the neighbouring industrial building and separated from it by a tall fence. The forecourt, bordered by water on two sides and regarded by the locals as their 'balcony' overlooking the area, is as much a playground for the schoolchildren, who also cross the street to use the more official neighbourhood playground a short way off. A strip of mosaic tiles, filled in by children from the school and given an enclosing edge of special stone tiles with tiny poems chiselled into them[12], marks the school's claim on this public zone, laid out by the local Public Works department, with a sandpit accessible to all the local children and, more recently, a climbing frame.

12 All these mosaic projects are based on ideas by Akelei Hertzberger who also offered to supervise their execution. On each occasion she stepped off from a general theme so as to frame and assemble so many individual contributions. This gave a communal, public component that drew together the welter of individuality into a single entity.

[4]

[5]

[6]

## Sandpit, De Koperwiek Primary School, Venlo, 1995-1997

The spiral shape of this sandpit gives it an open end. So rather than it being clear where the sand belongs, and where you expect it to stay, there is a gradual transition from brick to sand. Here, sweeping is a pointless occupation. The curving wall not only dominates the entire playground in terms of form but incites many activities there. The large egg-shapes and the prints of gigantic birds' feet in the seating wedges create the illusion that this huge primeval bird is actually there.[13]

13 Akelei Hertzberger was responsible for the idea, design and execution of the sandpit, eggs and birds' feet.

[1]

[2]

## De Opmaat Extended School, Arnhem, 2004-2007

To fend off protests by residents living opposite, the side of De Opmaat facing them has been designed as un-building-like as possible, more like a green hill in the school grounds.

This offered play potential normal enough in hilly terrain but quite exceptional in this polder-type landscape.

The main entrance for everyone except the youngest children is at the head of the broad stair. This stair acts as seating for a throng when there are events, as well as being an 'overstatement of accessibility'.

[3]

[4]

## Meerwijk Extended School, Haarlem, 2002-2007

With only a limited area to receive the combination of an Extended School and a substantial number of housing units, it was decided to make the dwellings reachable from the school roof. Hence this roof was made public street space and at the same time play space for the school and for the dwellings. Being so high up required the most gradual ascent possible, broken by a large landing. To the banisters are added, as inconspicuously as possible, the attributes of a climbing frame.

For the smallest children there is a ground floor patio reached directly from the schools. A crèche, a community centre and a gymnasium join the housing units on the raised street area, which has nothing left to remind one of a roof.

[1]

[2]

[3]

[4]

# Outdoor space

The habit still persists of siting schools freely in space, parked in green zones as it were, or in the non-existent centres of new residential areas. You would think that because of this midspace siting schools would possess great educational potential but the surface area is invariably kept to an absolute minimum and most of the green space around it is largely inaccessible 'visual greenery'.

There are of course schools, open-air schools for instance, in which working out of doors is a chosen special-priority theme where much thought is given to terraces off classrooms and even on occasion compound-like open-air classrooms set clear of the building. Generally, though, the school area beyond the actual building falls outside the sphere of education. Odd, when so many activities are ideally located outside, such as ones involving lots of water which gets spilt and sloshed around. Indeed, you can learn just as much outside as inside. For that, the customary artificial environment should be purposefully conditioned and cultivated into a testing ground for projects relating to biology, ecology, meteorology, geology and all the other ologies best enjoyed outside. Again, there is by no means always room for sports and certainly not football which seems restricted to the official club grounds only. You do come across school allotments and on the odd occasion animals for the children to look after, but facilities like these are vulnerable, particularly in the city, and really require roof terraces. Schools with special didactic methods are the only ones to devote time to 'natural' phenomena; in most other cases, the area round about is just an unsightly residual space, much like that left round a generally free-standing building to which the architect has given his all.

If there are advantages to a school sited independently, away from the residential environment, these are signally ignored. Not only does it take up an inordinate amount of land, it is unsafe for the children who have to travel relatively far to get there, and unsafe for the building, whose isolated setting makes it all too vulnerable. The vision of a tranquil school in a green setting is a far cry from urban reality.

[5]

[6]

# The schoolyard a street, the street a schoolyard

Playgrounds as they used to be, with their swarms of chattering children crammed to-gether behind iron railings, are best forgotten in the long run. Fences make the school an inviolable bastion that distances itself from the world. We see the school grounds being increasingly represented by an area giving directly onto the street. One fenced-in part is retained for the youngest children who might otherwise stray. This is impossible to combine with the more powerful dynamic of the older children. When schools are more open to the city, their outdoor area goes on to become part of the public domain and is open to everyone as a playground. Then one can imagine the line marking off the school territory to be more symbolic than functional, say little walls for sitting on, a demarcation instead of a fencing-in. The neighbourhood starts using the facilities which were initially meant for the schoolchildren, who in turn get more freedom of movement and more varied impressions.

The surface area and nature of a playground belonging to a school are scrupulously fixed by the authorities, but when the neighbourhood also uses it these aspects are open to negotiation which not infrequently opens up new avenues for the school in financial terms. The same holds for projects combining schools with housing. This gives the additional advantage of social control, of particular importance outside school hours.

As this housing shares the ground assigned to the school, we can share certain costs by planning wisely so that both parties benefit financially. This deal is favourable for the authorities and, providing we manage to tailor the design to it, for the school too. A mix of interests admittedly leads to a greater complexity but if well managed gives greater potential for all concerned.

The school's outdoor space becomes part of the street. With the demise of the fenced-in schoolyard the school becomes more integrated in the neighbourhood and in the city. The street in turn becomes part of the school's outdoor space.

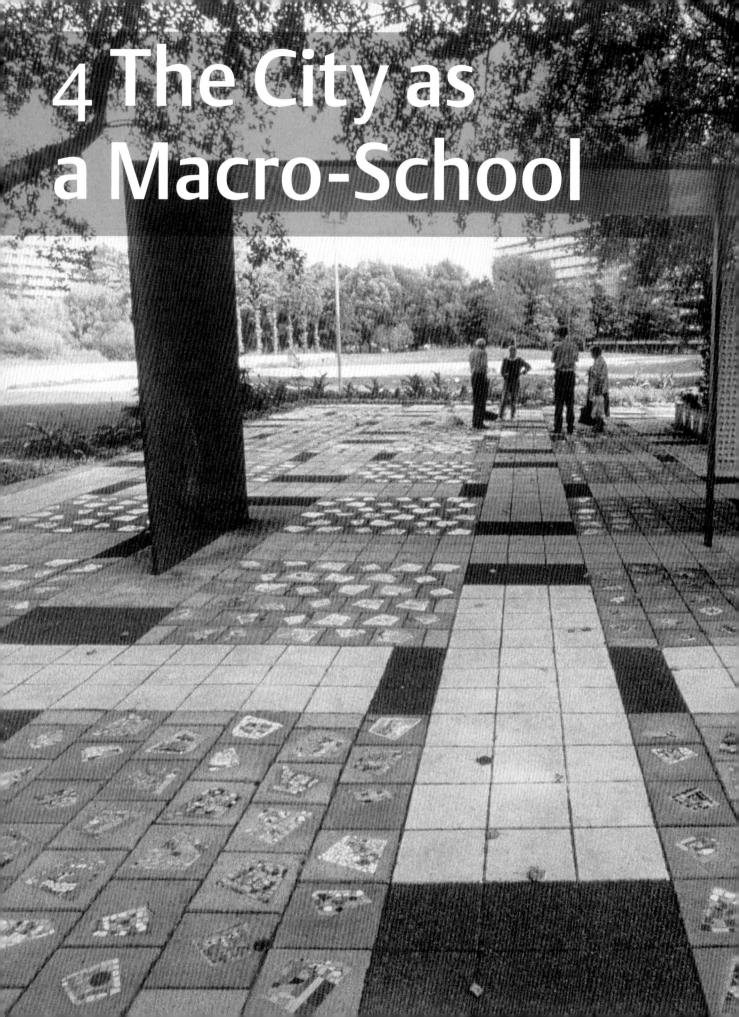

# 4 The City as a Macro-School

# The city as a macro-school

In the 1960s, the idea that education was a conservative institution that merely confirmed the established order took flight in the largely political statement that the only real lessons were to be learnt outside school. After all, everything has something to teach us; the philosopher and social critic Ivan Illich even felt that schools should be abolished altogether.[1] Clearly, there are two notions of what constitutes a school:

A a place to learn how well everything works so that you can later join in and help it all along;

B a place to learn to think for yourself so that you can form your own opinion of society.

As an institutionalized apparatus of tests, exams and canon formation, school can indeed be nothing other than a place where the values and standards to be upheld resound, confirming the established order, and in that sense it is conservative.

The sixties unleashed a torrent of criticism of a bankrupt education, in particular at the universities, in an aftershock of disappointment once it was clear that the Second World War, for all the ideas and talk about freedom, had failed to change a thing.

The student uprising, which in the summer of 1968 in the universities and in the streets of Paris looked like becoming a real revolution, spread to most other universities of the world. Everywhere, the place and responsibility of the university as intellectual motor of a more democratic society were called into question.

*One-Dimensional Man* (1964) written by the philosopher Herbert Marcuse describes how an increasingly powerful and affluent capitalism would reduce people to consumer slaves until they were themselves consumed by their own system. In his book Marcuse describes how all thinking is corrupted by interests that at first sight appear advantageous but would ultimately lead to an inability to think for ourselves and a general anaesthetizing of our growth. The only ones able to divert this development, according to Marcuse, were the students. Only they were still in a position to think independently, not yet being caught up in the nets of the establishment. This call was certainly a key motivating factor in the ferment among students who were further galvanized into action by Marxists and Maoists, part of a heterogeneous assemblage of young left-wingers, all in their own way out to reform the existing order, usually for political

[2] "Society is a carnivorous flower"

◄ [1] Monument to the victims of the plane crash in Bijlmermeer, Amsterdam

reasons. Although the students had varied intentions and differed in degrees of radi-
cality, they were united in the conviction that the existing school system should go
and that universities should be drastically democratized.

Development should mean more than just scaling the social ladder, every one of
whose rungs was programmed or prescribed beforehand, making it impossible to devi-
ate and still be admitted on the next rung up. Everyone should be able to develop, not
just an elite with the funds at its disposal. Otherwise perhaps we *should* abolish schools
altogether.

Ivan Illich's concept of 'deschooling' society, meant for the the poorest parts of South
America, was more than anything else a political statement. And even though good
education is still an illusion in much of the world, Illich's ideas seem dated now.

[1]

Although now stripped of its original radical nature, the wave of democratization
sweeping the 1960s is in many ways still the mainstay of thinking about another kind
of education and another kind of school. Learning, generally speaking, has steadily been
loosening itself from the classroom-based autonomous school model and has broken
out of its traditional cage.

Today's society might be described as a 'knowledge class society'. There is a quality
war on among courses and places of study and at the same time, maybe in reaction to
this, an increased attention to development within a wider spectrum of cultural and
societal prospects as initiated along a broad front in the 1960s.

[2]

In propagating the idea of *éducation permanente* – that is, viewing life as a continuous
learning programme, in or out of school – the classrooms are opened to those other
than the regular pupils, people of all ages who would like to go back to school and
those deprived of that opportunity first time round. This possibility to continue learning
adds to the awareness that it is not just the time spent at school that defines your
development, but that that development continues throughout your life.

'Learning in the street' is a new paradigm that has since made its way into modern
education. If education at the modern school spills out of the classroom into learning
streets and learning squares, at the Extended School education automatically extends
its territory since it includes local facilities, which means having to interact with others.
Whenever we architects succeed in creating at least the spatial conditions for this, we
see learning spilling out past the confines of the school grounds and into the city.
Schools don't stop at their outer walls – or rather, those outer walls are unable to stem
the flow of learning.

1  Ivan Illich, *Deschooling Society*, Open Forum, London: Calder and
   Boyars, 1971

# Public void or public space

The city is a network of links between people and organizations of an unparalleled intensity, a brain as it were with a collective memory and with a singularity and a personality of its own whose qualities are strengthened over time. A school is another such brain, only smaller and less complex. Common to city and school is their social character, as a community in which everyone's ideas and opinions are conveyed to each other by a wide variety of contacts in a large and multi-branched network.

It is up to architects and urban planners to give shape to the space for community, both inside and outside. What matters most is the space of the street, what we call public space (just how public is public and whether this term says enough is another matter). Architects have to turn 'public space' into 'social space', space tailored to exchange where one confers with and is measured against others; space invested with meaning for its occupants by events there, now and in the past, and the experiences these events have yielded.

It takes more to turn public space into social space than simply imitating the romantic images of old towns with their multiplicity of places, their seclusion and their nearness – an impracticable task anyway.

The reality of the situation is as follows:

- there are ever-increasing numbers of parked or moving cars that threaten to clog the entirety of urban space, which requires widening the streets with, as a result,
- buildings so far apart due to too many cars, rules about sunlighting, cycle paths and other divisions of duties, that they lack the necessary cohesion so that there is noth-

[3]

[4]

ing whatsoever of the interior quality we value so highly in old town centres, and, consequently,

- excessively low development and population densities;
- dwellings of such comfort as to alleviate the need to look for this commodity in the streets;
- our heavily diminished dependence on one another due to our increased affluence and individuality;
- few collective events to fill out the public space and give it meaning except in isolated instances;
- degeneration of the notion of street as a result of vandalism and physical decay, a real problem in places but on the whole exaggerated. This negative picture is all too often aggravated by bad planning and poor designs (indeed, the lack of effective management by the authorities shows yet again that tackling it is not regarded as a priority issue);
- the potentials of virtual encounter on the internet, because of which people have less need to hit the streets to feel part of a 'group'.

Public space, or what passes for it, generally speaking has become foreign to a city's inhabitants. Who still feels attracted to public space, and who knows what to make of it? In reality there is no independent physical seat of social life these days, which means there is no social life in spatial terms. Of course there are stadiums, theatres, discos, shopping centres and stations, eulogized by many as the modern, protected, secure fairytale palaces of commerce as a replacement for the often dilapidated public realm. All these buildings may succeed in sustaining large numbers of people and inciting a degree of togetherness, but social spaces they are not. People have little or no influence on the course of events: they are being guided rather than doing the guiding themselves. That much of urban life is increasingly being enacted inside, that is, in free-standing objects resembling large containers, is not itself the problem; rather, it is that the excessively open zones for traffic or parkland remaining *outside* are steadily losing their meaning over time, leading to junk space.

If the meaning of public space as social space is lost, we are left with public void. Architects and urban planners must spend less time making buildings look good and devote their attention and energy to what is it that belongs between those buildings: meaningful social space.

# Redesign of Museumplein, Amsterdam, 1999
## Sven-Ingvar Andersson

The strange phenomenon given the name Ezelsoor ('the donkey's ear') seems to have arisen out of a typical urban planning conflict in which an underground supermarket needed an entrance at a place in the square (Museumplein) designated as public space. Prominent intellectuals, artists and architects vigorously protested at the time against this ham-fisted, brash solution which upset plans to give prominence to the forthcoming extension to the Stedelijk Museum. Who at that time would have predicted that this unfortunate element of

Sven-Ingvar Andersson's landscape design, almost universally vilified and considered to be of secondary importance anyway, would eventually become the busiest place in the entire square? Located along the bustling street, opposite the Concertgebouw, at the entrance to a parking facility with the supermarket next door – all this is reason enough for it to be the busiest part. Elevating the otherwise entirely flush square at this point has produced something of a hill from where you can look out over the square. If there is anything on in Museumplein, how-

ever trifling, this area is packed and has something of a grandstand. Not just that, its favourable orientation makes it an ideal place to catch some sun.

All these qualities distinguish this corner from the rest of the square so that it attracts more attention than many another place designed with much more subtle means. Its marked presence at such a strategic place in the square and its spectacular quality make it a focal point in social terms too.

Before, the square used to be sliced in two

[1]

[2]

[3]

[1]

[4]  Tuilleries Pool, Paris
(photo from 1978)

[2]

lengthwise by an ultra-brief though broad and busy motorway from which you had to deflect to the left or right before reaching the Rijksmuseum. After the makeover it was replaced by a continuous lawn with a large and well-used play pool on axis with the museum. Its broad low edge makes a wonderful transition to the water and can be used for sitting and very often lying on. It is just such urban design details that show how well the designer has understood the future patterns of use here, whether in summer or in winter when you can get your skates out of storage. The large expanse of grass does duty as a venue for pop and classical concerts, demonstrations and other large-scale events, possible since the makeover and now taken for granted by everyone. As for the demise of the traffic route, it's long forgotten now.

[3]

[4]

[1]

[2]

# Cities for children

There is precious little heed paid to children in the public realm and what space there is, often has little to offer them. Only a fraction of the space is really and truly suitable for children. It seems we simply don't consider them important enough. Administrators and urban planners presumably are more interested in economic needs, and plan masses of green space to compensate. Green stands for peace and quiet and the more the population ages, the more votes it will get. Investing in the adults of the future evidently means having to wait too long for results.

Children when away from home and school are expected to behave like adults and keep to the rules that generally apply. The sooner they learn these, the safer they will be. Outmoded methods of education preside here. Space for young people, whether left over or designed, is scattered about wherever convenient in the form of play areas for toddlers. Very occasionally, there is a goal where mainly older boys can play football after a fashion. For the rest, there are of course playgrounds, recreation areas, (supervised) football fields. Usually located far from home, the children have to make an effort to go there or be brought.
Again, any leftover or vacant urban land that has been spontaneously appropriated by children to play football or just play gets built up sooner or later, so that the few football pitches left are steadily retreating towards the city outskirts.

Without wanting to play down in any way the problems in the major cities with older children and their sporadic outbursts of frustration, it is clear that the inadequacies of urban planning have an underestimated part in it. There should simply be more space for skating, playing football and other sports and sports-related activities, at the expense of a little green space if necessary. After all, youngsters can relate better to asphalt especially if there are bumps and hollows in it. And there was no mistaking the message conveyed by those small children who paid the required amount into a parking metre to 'hire' an area the size of a car to build a house for their dolls, to the utter consternation of motorists frantically looking for a place to park.
The fenced-off facilities planned specially for the slightly older children remind one most of reservations, protected and protective zones for an exclusive and vulnerable minority. By offering the children a Utopia of sorts, thereby throwing the 'tough' city into relief, the difference between them and adults is inappropriately stressed yet again.
These days, the only streets left for children to play in, with all the unexpected and exciting adventures this entails, are those of the quiet but often all too dull suburbs. For the older boys with their boundless energy who want to show what they are made of and practice their skills there are few facilities, if any.
People live in cities because cities have the greatest conceivable choice and variety and the ultimate in things to do. The notion of public nuisance has little meaning there. There's always the country if it's peace and quiet you want. This is not a call for chaos, but for a more dynamic order of a greater complexity.
The need for security and peace and quiet are typical mainstream pleasures belonging in a static society where the individual interests of the well-heeled are uppermost, with no mind for the development of the community as a whole and its dynamics.

If we regard space for young people and its potential for their development as a thermometer to measure the state of play in the public realm, that is, its riches and prospects, then this is a call for organizing that public realm along different lines; not disordered but with more leeway. It is at the same time an appeal to architects and planners to address the situation with greater passion.

In the modern city everything is planned, without a single snippet of land managing to sneak past the planners. Everything has been giving something useful to do, consistent with the all-embracing established order, a fine-meshed net of rules, technological systems and health and safety measures trawling our environment; everything has to be predictable and manageable so that no unforeseen situations can crop up. Any margin or room to manoeuvre is banned by the system. Leftover and unallocated places soon become hookup spots for the local youth. Given the negative implications they undeniably have, such places are soon stigmatized, then sterilized and lastly given a more decent designation with all speed. The more obvious choice of a relational challenge, so essential if there is to be social cohesion, is eliminated from the start.

"The net of rules and standards is drawing ever tighter in its definition of what is strictly necessary; that is, accommodating it in fixed meanings. Space is categorically excluded from the signified in that definition, and it is just this space of the indeterminate, the unexpected, the informal, the unofficial, that architects should be taking care of.
"Space, then, is that which manages to escape the confines of the established, the specified, the regulated, the official and so is there for the taking and open to interpretation. The idea of space stands for everything that widens or removes existing limitations and for everything that opens up more possibilities, and is thus the opposite of hermetic, oppressing, awkward, shut up and divided up into drawers and partitions, sorted, established, predetermined and immutable, shut in, made certain. Most of all, space is between, the thing that building leaves free, and that requires a radical shift in focus."[2]
What we here call 'space' is comparable with 'learning' as opposed to 'education'. Education is instruction in the so-called required subject matter. Learning, by contrast, is about the space left over or open outside the institutionalized paths: the space of the in-between, of the as yet undetermined. New discoveries, possibilities, images and experiences arise precisely by looking along and therefore beyond what is already defined, that which is established. Perhaps we might be able to live in an entirely regimented and defined world where everything is static. But there would be nothing new to learn, beyond the acknowledged ways. And with each sliver of land marked off and labelled, the room for discovery and adventure is itself smothered by our mania for regulating everything, being at best the official play space, arranged and established and therefore impervious to new experiences and interpretations.

And what do children experience on their way to school? Does their route there have anything to offer, or for them to discover? And what is there to experience of the world besides the hazards of traffic? Do they pass intriguing shops, attractive or ugly buildings, markets, monuments, statues, art? Do they experience anything of work being done, companies, professions? Does the road lead past a variety of streets, water, boats, a place to swim, anglers, animals, through a park, past trees you can climb, and are there different routes to choose from that vary these experiences? Where can they play football or skate?

The experiences children in particular absorb from the city are their most important source of education besides what they learn at home and officially at school.

• We should see to it that nothing becomes more abstract, large-scale and therefore more alienated than is absolutely necessary.

• We should not be party to barring or erasing the activity of companies and organizations branded as a public nuisance merely to submit to the overwhelming ascendancy of order and peace-and-quiet fanatics out to lull residential areas to sleep.

• We must prevent powerful economic forces from snubbing out small shops, often set up by immigrants and with a wide variety of wares on offer, by making deals with the authorities.

• In short, we should do everything to bring city, school and home into alignment and make of them one seamless world of experience. This is a job for urban planners and architects.

2  *Lessons* 2, pp. 211, 14

Fireplug in New York, USA, 1969

# Playgrounds

Essentially, the 'playground' phenomenon is an indication that cities are themselves
unable to provide enough, if any, of the quality that makes children feel at home and
encourages their development. Broken-up streets, say to renew wastepipes or carry
out construction work of some sort, have always appealed to children more than the
conditioned circumstances of a playground. So specially devised places for children to
play, such as those designed by Aldo van Eyck, can be regarded as prostheses for an
inadequate city, a city that takes no account of a large share of its population. But it is
the outstanding quality of Van Eyck's designs that simultaneously made them urban
design, architecture and art and this is what justified their presence.

This cannot be said of the bewildering array of mainly wooden play accessories that
sprang up everywhere in their wake, most of them in vivid undifferentiated colours.
Admittedly attractive to children, their intended realistic forms are utterly incapable
of firing the imagination. These sad products with their invariably overcomplicated
and garish appearance roll in an endless stream from the mountain of catalogues
launched by a trade evidently not that concerned about what might stimulate children's development. There are of course peerless inventions such as slides, skate
courses and large complex climbing structures designed with great sensitivity and an
understanding of the particular needs of the different age groups. But all too often you
get dodgy-looking metal structures resembling medieval instruments of torture with
lots of fencing that seems to hold the children prisoner, which only strengthens the
associations with deprivation of freedom.

[1]

[1] Gibraltarstraat, Kijkduinstraat,
Amsterdam, 1953

[2] Slide, Berlin

[3] Halfpipe

[4] Carve, De Windvang,
Scheveningen, 2002

[2]

[3]

[4]

[1] Slide designed by artist Carsten Höller as part of an exhibition in Tate Modern, London, 2006 (photo: AP)

The government is lessening its influence on the choice of play equipment. This is increasingly being left to those most directly concerned, and although this may seem sensible it does mean that these parties, not being particularly well versed in the subject, all too easily opt for what looks good – the industry knows best! Actually, more and more designers are making playgrounds their focus. We increasingly see parts of the city being fitted out specially for children, artificial worlds resembling reservations that are both inappropriate and insubstantial, without the children learning how to engage with their city and without the city learning to take its children seriously.

In the meantime, safety regulations are being systematically tightened, not so much because of accidents regularly occurring, at least not to our knowledge, but most probably because a more assertive public has brought an increase in liability claims, which in turn only aggravates fears of unsafe conditions. There is no end to the measures that could be devised to satisfy an excessively sensitive government. If it keeps on like this, our hands will soon be completely tied.

## Play place
### Raymond Hirs and P. Breed

This facility was made for the nearby school, but the surroundings suggest a park setting, embedded in the grass, a place where differences in height need reconciling.
The spiral shape acts as a magnet and draws people together; an inviting gesture at its most basic.
The steps suggest places to sit and the centre makes an obvious play area open to all.

This basic intervention is a confirmation of place as it searches for the centre, like a whirlpool drawing the attention of its surroundings to it. A clearing in the landscape, it is in effect the theatre of Epidaurus in miniature.

Curiously, this supremely architectural task was achieved by artists, who here showed themselves to have more architecture in their heads and hands than most architects, who in turn are always dreaming about making art.

[2]

[3]

[4]

## Playgrounds for Amsterdam Public Works, 1947-1978
## Aldo van Eyck

In 1947 Aldo van Eyck joined the employ of Amsterdam Public Works to give form to an impressive programme of playgrounds spread throughout the city. The initiative for this enterprise came from Jacoba Mulder, head of the municipal urban planning department, under the supervision of Cornelis van Eesteren.

Aldo van Eyck designed a number of fixed elements: sandpits, climbing racks, railings, seats and stepping-jumping-sitting stones. This range was extended and varied over the years. For each playground Van Eyck designed a new composition of these elements, so that each place had its own unique setting. They were invariably located at sites on the edge of town, dilapidated and leftover areas in the inner city, and excessively large empty corners in the suburbs.

The play elements were thoughtfully designed, keeping in mind what it is that children find exciting, in primary forms and materials with no colours added. There was

[1]

[2]

[3]

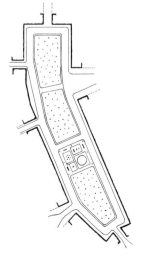

[4]

one exception to this, the playground at Zeedijk where he worked with the artist Joost van Roojen who transformed, as only an artist can, the edge of a condemned area into the fantasy of a new world for the city and its children. It was a literal example of what Van Eyck was calling for in his essay 'The Child, the City and the Artist'.[3] The quality and success of the scores of many simple, abstract playgrounds designed by Aldo van Eyck with elements that included street furniture, lay in their primary form, open to the imaginations of children and oriented to their motor development.

Some 700 playgrounds were deployed across Amsterdam, in general as central as possible in residential areas and so closest to home. After all, they were meant for the very youngest children, although the climbing frames were quite a challenge even for the older ones. Nearly all these playgrounds have now gone, most of them having fallen into disrepair due to poor upkeep and then declared unsafe by recent standards and dismantled.

With his playgrounds, Aldo van Eyck showed in inimitable fashion how architects can make an essential contribution to the public realm. Of his entire body of work, the playgrounds attest best to the convincing and resolute approach by the authorities of the 1950s, '60s and '70s. Unfortunately it also makes painfully clear how thoroughly these same authorities have lost the plot since those enlightened times.

3 Aldo van Eyck, 'The child, the city and the artist', 1962, unpublished manuscript

[1] Zeedijk playground with wall painting by Joost van Roojen

[2-4] Zaanhof, Amsterdam

## BasketBar, Utrecht, 2001-2002 | wos 8 heat transfer station, Utrecht, 1997-1998 | Leerpark, Dordrecht, 2004-2006    NL Architects

NL Architects were commissioned to design a small café cum bar, in tandem with an existing bookshop which was to be enlarged, at the epicentre of student coming and going in the heart of De Uithof, the campus of Utrecht University. Important though this café most certainly is in this academic world, its relatively small size made it no match architecturally for its burly neighbours. This certainly held for the reticent

form NL Architects chose. So they shifted the dominant feature of the project to the roof. By fitting this out as a basketball pitch, they gave an entirely new slant to the project and an appeal easily equal to that of the bar below.

This basketball roof is not only open to students, and with a busstop right at the door young people come from far and wide, constantly in search as they are of one of

those few places designed with them in mind, where they can enjoy their favourite pastime without disturbing others or being disturbed.

Architecturally speaking, a flat roof would not have been out of place here, but the added practical value has enriched the social pattern of this place immensely. With the café floor set a metre or so lower than the surrounding street level, you enter by

[1]

[2]

way of a sitting/surfing hollow, which at some places is an extension of the bar and at others is populated by kids from the street looking for confrontation and conflict, so characteristic of social space in the public realm. Here the space of the city is deliberately galvanized and made approachable and accessible. And so this modest building manages to withstand the surrounding brick inferno, attracting most of the attention and pepping up the place enormously.

At a transfer station in Utrecht, in principle an unassailable bastion inside which you have no business, the outer walls were provided with climbing grips to make them touchy-feely and climbable, for young people in other words. It illustrates the principle of making the world less abstract and more accessible, using architecture to enable us to experience more in and of that world.

When designing a sports building in Dordrecht NL Architects made a veritable rockface of the street facades that must be difficult for arriving sports enthusiasts to resist.

Buildings given this additional challenging quality are less aloof and lose their impregnability, becoming part of the street in more senses than one.

[1] BasketBar

[2] Climbing wall, Leerpark, Dordrecht

[3] WOS 8 heat transfer station, Utrecht

[3]

## 'Playscape', Quartier Salengro, Drancy, France, 2003
## Massimo Ciuffini with Luca La Torre, Ketty Di Tardo, Alberto Lacovoni, Francesco Careri and Alexander Valentino

In 2003, the French site for the 7th Europan competition was the Salengro quarter at Drancy. The brief called for proposals to retain and renovate the bare concrete social housing blocks, as found in *banlieux* throughout France. These so-called HLM's (Habitation à Loyer Modéré) are now often more that fifty years old and to all intents and purposes obsolete. The units are too small and technically flawed.

In the proposal by Massimo Ciuffini and his colleagues, codename Playscape, the housing blocks are wrapped in a zone of light-weight construction that can be filled in as an extension, a new skin and insulation. The immediate surroundings of the block are asphalted. Craters and humps in the asphalt make it a landscape for skating and for working up with chalk.

In the first place, this project adopts a serious stance towards the existing, using it and expanding upon it. It also shows an entirely different but perhaps more realistic attitude to the living environment where normally speaking the idea of an idyll of tranquility in a leafy environment still prevails. Playscape refrains from emphasizing the green of its setting. At first, the Europan jury was unimpressed because it had so little green space. It was only after intense deliberation that it began to dawn on them that this might signal a new understanding of the issue, with a greater focus on expanding the potential for young people. So in Playscape the living environment is interpreted primarily as a place to play and not sacrificed to the customary obsession with green space.

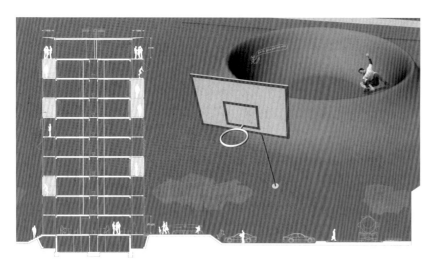

[1]

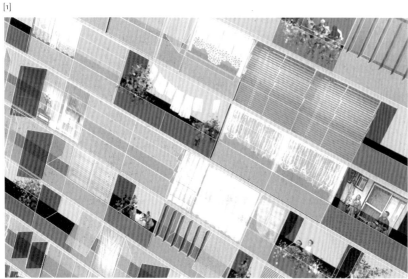

[2]

[3]

[4]

# Sandpits

Sandpits are irreplaceable. Their possibilities are endless and incite exploration by children at all stages of development. Although everyone agrees on this, the construction and use of sandpits is increasingly subject to criticism and getting them in place is becoming more and more difficult if not impossible. Once there were letters from people complaining about sand blowing into their homes; now we see increasing resistance to sandpits because of their unhygienic aspects, as if these were something new. The point is whether or not you're willing to accept them. Fences and coverings to keep out cats, dogs and rain together with anti-worm pills should counter all objections. Public Works for their part are increasingly averse to the need to periodically change the sand. So sandpits are the subject of criticism and regarded as a burden and hence are losing popularity even though there is no real alternative. Happily there are places like Amsterdam where the sandpits keep coming, while they continue to disappear elsewhere.

[5]

[6]

[7]

As sandpits are usually populated by the very youngest children who need to be accompanied by adults, there are always benches alongside them. If we realize that these are the ideal places (and maybe the only places in the city) for shy immigrants to engage with the indigenous population, even if only a question of keeping an eye on each other's children, we cannot deny the importance for the community of such meeting places.

Such social fraternalizing is nowhere as successful as here. This fact alone should be reason enough to take a less lackadaisical and disparaging attitude to sandpits. Beyond that, at the sandpit children are confronted with each other's presence and claims to a single territory. The conflicts this can give rise to have to be resolved by talking it through and cooperating. Sandpits are like social arenas where situations from the great big world are played out first. If we observe children playing with sand – endlessly scooping it up, emptying it out, making mud pies – it doesn't take a developmental psychologist to conclude that besides social skills they are exercising motor skills in the most effective way imaginable.

[1]

[2]

[1, 2] Lindenstrasse and Markgraf-strasse residential court, Berlin, 1986. The large sandpit forming the hub of this residential court was built by the residents together, led by Akelei, featuring edges in mosaic inspired by illustrations of work by Gaudí and Jujol.

► [3] Aldo van Eyck, playground with wall painting by Joost van Roojen, Zeedijk, Amsterdam: meeting place for parents (photo SemPresser/MAI)

[1]

## 'Dessous les pavés c'est la plage'

The largest and most adventurous sandpit occurs whenever the road is dug up. Then the cars have to relinquish their dominating and space-devouring position and the street temporarily becomes the domain of children who are briefly freed from the iron walls of shiny monsters that are not to be touched and that separate the two sides of the street.

"We have got used to this absurd situation, and we seem to have resigned ourselves to children no longer being able to go to school alone, and it even being dangerous for them to play outside. Every day more asphalt is brought into our cities: more and more accessibility, but also fewer and fewer places to go.

"But when a drainage system happens to need renewing, it is like a sort of miracle happening. The cars are kept at bay, and the consequence is a big sandpit full of playing children. Where are those children at other times, when, as is normal, the drainpipes are not being renewed? Suddenly the contact between the two sides of the street is reinstated to what it must formerly have been: the street not as a barrier, but as the cement joining the houses."4

4 Herman Hertzberger, 'Homework for more hospitable form', in *Forum* XXIV no. 3, 1973

# Play space

Space to play, undesignated or marginal space, should be present as an evident quality of every residential setting and of the public domain as a whole, as evident as children themselves. It is quite impossible to imagine children developing their play skills exclusively at specially allocated places with equipment specially devised for the purpose, that is, set apart from everything in our normal daily living environment. It is this need to get things in order, for functionality and efficiency that sees to it that everything is narrowed down to one particular purpose, the ultimate consequence being that each thing is only suited to that one simple limited task. This way, the distinction between what is good for youngsters, adults and old people is magnified and then consolidated. So we see the public realm split into so many fragments, each suited to its purpose but to that purpose alone.

Playgrounds and play equipment may be better than nothing, but designed as single-purpose appliances they can be used in just the one way. They give little or no incentive to be used otherwise. The playgrounds designed by Aldo van Eyck composed from basic elements are peerless in firing the imagination. Paradoxically, it is these outstanding examples that increase the doubts attendant on such facilities.

Equipment intended for one purpose only presupposes its users to be passive consumers that need putting at their ease. In the meantime, daily life depends entirely upon vast numbers of such single-purpose facilities. However, we should constantly question whether we are to continue on automatic pilot this way or at some point be able to decide things for ourselves.

[2]

This is made clear by the difference between an appliance or apparatus, and an instrument. "Form directed towards a given purpose functions as an apparatus, and where form and programme are mutually evocative the apparatus itself becomes an instrument. A properly functioning apparatus does the work for which it is programmed, that which is expected of it – no less, but also no more. By pressing the right buttons the expected results are obtained, the same for everyone, always the same.

"A (musical) instrument essentially contains as many possibilities of usage as uses to which it is put – an instrument must be played. Within the limits of the instrument, it is up to the player to draw what he can from it, within the limits of his own ability. Thus instrument and player reveal to each other their respective abilities to complement and fulfill one another. Form as an instrument offers the scope for each person to do what he has most at heart, and above all to do it in his own way."[5]

For things to possess the quality of an instrument they must be interpretable in more than one way, enabling them to accept (and reject) multiple uses and multiple meanings; not everyone sees things the same or gets the same out of them. So there needs to be a margin, room for a wealth of experiences contingent on the person, their objective and the situation at hand.

[1] Entrance stair on Churchilllaan, Amsterdam

If we were to grasp the opportunity to build such play space into everything we designed, we could free the city from its tenacious monofunctional constriction, which is only increasing because of the fear of losing control. So here it's about the space's ability to be 'played' as an implicit quality of the city, in other words about more informal 'room' between formal designations. We find space for discovery and learning where things are not governed by clarity, such as in only partially defined or undesignated contexts. And this is without even considering obscure spots, abandoned buildings, forgotten corners, alleyways, buildings fallen into disuse whose original meaning is lost to us.

It makes a big difference what kind of neighbourhood you grew up in; whether the environment was rife with stimuli and experiences but also whether there were intriguing items in the streets and on the houses that occupied you, puzzled you or opened your eyes to something.

Adventure sounds out the limits, increases the margin. Play space is mainly found among what is official and functionally necessary, in other words among the established meaning of specified functions. Neighbourhoods that are rich in appeal and associations are the ones full of special places, copses, trees to climb, water, walls or relics of former times, and where the buildings on the street have elements with play potential such as porches, bays or corners. Everyone has their own examples and memories from childhood, and these may even be of lifelong influence.

One of my earliest memories is of the stone egg-shapes in the street terminating the outdoor stairs. As a child you were made to sit on them, and the feeling this gave you remained. For even though these ornaments had almost no architectural significance, they made the houses solid, approachable, near, qualities that clearly reach out to a small child, imperceptibly instilling a feeling of trust and lessening the threat of the great big world. There was also that place under a bay window where you just managed to fit, in the knowledge that soon you would be too big for it. Just such recesses, protuberances, ledges and edges made the building measurable, more accessible, more inviting.

5  Herman Hertzberger, 'Homework for more hospitable form', in *Forum* XXIV no. 3, 1973, pp. 12-13

## Roof of Unité d'Habitation, Marseille, 1947-1952
## Le Corbusier

This roof was painstakingly designed by Le Corbusier as a landscape-like public realm for children but equally for adults. All forms, benches, walls for changing behind, a raked surface to sunbathe on, have been considered in every detail. Actually, the only clearly defined component of this roof is the paddling pool. "All these facilities and the form they are given attest to an abiding attention to the inviting nature of the form which for Le Corbusier always automatically takes pride of place before its sculptural expression."[6]

Remarkably, nothing gives the impression of having been designed as play equipment. Their applications speak for themselves, or rather, they are brought out naturally by the children. These forms evidently are capable of evoking associations without in any way illustrating these explicitly.

6 *Lessons* 2, p. 82

[2]

[3]

[4]

**Stair at rue Vilin, Belleville, Paris**
Photo by Willy Ronis, 1959

"There is clearly more involved here than just the concrete stair, a construction in its own right joining the lower-lying neighbourhood to that higher up. ... Here at this place, where the layers of the metropolis come to light in a pocket edition, there is real freedom of movement. It makes a vigorous contrast with the desolate perspective of the none-too-exciting street above. Not designed for this purpose and without explicitly offering the opportunity for it, this marginal spot is a place where children can get together undisturbed."[7] This undedicated leftover space designed for no particular purpose, away from the official and unambiguous stairs, has a strong pull on these children. It must be its unknown, risky and unpredictable quality that puts them in their element.

7 *Lessons 2*, p. 272

## Temples, Bali

Multiple use of space is by no means unknown in our culture, but it is not second nature to us either. In our thinking, things and their uses are generally fixed, subjugated within a particular category or system of meanings.

At many places on the island of Bali there are groups of small temples, wooden huts on stone bases that seem not to be in use.[8] They only take on a purpose and meaning when temporarily decorated and furnished as temples for certain ceremonies. When deprived of this status, they are receptive to children at play who let their imaginations loose on them. This is just one example of how children can be fired and challenged by their surroundings, and of how they appropriate those surroundings.

8 See *Lessons for Students in Architecture*, pp. 104-106

[2]

[3]

## Street railing

For children, any fence or railing in the street[9] makes the most natural climbing frame. It might even make a tent on occasion.

This additional quality was never intentional, unlike the climbable walls of NL Architects (see p. 221), but is due to the associations evoked by this railing's elementary form.

9  See *Lessons for Students in Architecture*, p. 178

[1]

[2]

## Ibirapuera Pavilion, São Paulo, 1951
## Oscar Niemeyer with Helio Uchoa and Joaqim Cardozo

The pavilion Oscar Niemeyer designed for Ibirapuera park in São Paulo is an expansive concrete slab stretched like a canvas between the four buildings also designed by him along the periphery. This pavilion makes for a shaded pedestrian throughway. Below this concrete slab, exceedingly broad at the centre and tapering at the extremities and snaking between the green areas, can be found a number of built cores that include a small gallery and a restaurant. The floor follows the curving periphery of the roof above it and consists of a smooth layer of cement which gives on all sides onto the gravel in the park. At the restaurant, this floor doubles as a limitless terrace in the shade. Although it is almost inconceivable that Niemeyer thought of this, it is an eldorado for skaters who express the spaciousness of this built statement with their audacious long, fast displays. Its construction using a minimum number of columns and invisible beams will not have been without its problems, but this lightweight elegant gesture reveals nothing of it. The expansive pavilion is the stone heart of the park, its minimal conditions offering alongside the generous terrace a super-dynamic practice area mainly for active youngsters amidst the greenery. This is an eloquent example of meaningful public space.

[3]

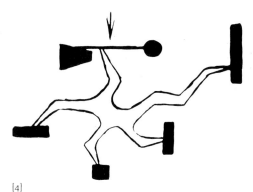

[4]

[5]

[1] Northern France

[2] New York, 1950
(photo William Klein)

# The Learning City

Our 'city for children' is a wake-up call not only to attend more to this vulnerable group, particularly where road safety is concerned, but at the same time to make more space for a group that is dynamic and inquiring and not always in step. Back in 1962 Aldo van Eyck in his essay 'The child, the city and the artist' contended that the unsuitability of the modern city for children calls into question its suitability for everyone.

It is children that lay bare the fundamental unfitness of an order and layout largely grounded in political and economic interests, and therefore primarily opportunist by nature. If we want a city that opens our eyes and contributes to developing and activating people instead of staking everything on a meek, smooth-running, settled life we had better take young people and their needs as a yardstick for public space. The city for children is a better departure-point for the city for everyone.

If we are to be more mindful of what children may expect of the city as their environment, we must look at what we make more through their eyes. Not that the alternative city this gives us is not good for grown-ups. There may be differences between young and old, big and small, but the 'world of the child' is the same world as that of adults. There is no clear age boundary between child and adult; they are the same animal, inseparable from and dependent upon one another. Children are not subject to metamorphosis the way a caterpillar changes into a butterfly. The adult is already present in the child and everything you acquire as a child will guide and pursue you as an adult. Nor is there a special measure for children, let alone a scale. Of course there are differences in size, but we all live in the same world and we all have to climb the same stairs with the same risers.

So in principle children's needs are illustrative of everyone else's. What is good for children is good for everybody. You never stop absorbing new experiences. The Learning City makes no distinction between children and grown-ups.

Every experience is the stuff of learning. Learning is like eating and drinking and we all do that, only children are often greedier and tend to drink in everything they hear and see. All the impressions they get, experiences they have and information they acquire are imported into the existing order of the brain. They have to be incorporated into the child's familiar world, expanding and confirming it to get a better grasp of the world at large.

If the brain as an internal city is an impression of the external city, then the ideal external city should have the most richly varied environment; a city that is nowhere dull, dry or bleak, nor hermetically defined and ultra-safe, but rather a place where you have to hold your ground and watch your step. Of course there are negative experiences to be had in a city. Living there you are automatically exposed to these; all the more reason to counter them with as broad a front as possible.

A city is a Learning City when it arouses our curiosity, draws us in, a place where discoveries are to be made, that invites associations, stimulates thinking.

The Learning City is a new paradigm which states that administrators *and* designers of modern cities should focus more fully on other criteria when giving shape to space. It's not just about purchasing power and consumer activity, but more the contribution public space makes to our development and to an understanding of the world and of

◄ Steps of Columbia University, New York, USA, Charles Follen McKim 1894

each other's motives and actions. To this end, the criteria for designing that space have to become less concerned with the short-term, less hedonistic, less consumption-driven and less self-centred. Over time, modern residential areas are becoming increasingly dominated by relaxation, solitude and safety and obsessed with green space. There is precious little there to stimulate the mind, especially for children.

street | stairs as in-between zone | building

When learning goes beyond being a process of adapting children to the world of grown-ups and when all the things we experience passively and actively become a form of learning (when development since the Age of Enlightenment is regarded as the universal motor of life), the distinction between children and adults in terms of the city is reduced to almost nil. Even so, children are more vulnerable, less able to see their way there and less able to stand up for their interests and needs.

Instead of the current set-up where children are automatically expected to adapt to the criteria of their elders, we could take the reverse situation. The space in a city, when tailored to its young people gives that city a firmer basis from which to proceed, equipped as it is for a permanent learning process for all its inhabitants: a Learning City.

The idea of *éducation permanente* ('learning for life') dislodges learning from the limitations of a fixed school curriculum for a particular age group. This elevates mental development to a universal theme, the daily practice we all deal with constantly, regardless of age. This not only unhitches learning from immaturity and opens up the school to all ages but presupposes an awareness of the fundamental boundlessness of learning and of continuous development. With learning no longer limited by age or time, logically our entire living space as learning space becomes the spatial equivalent of an *éducation permanente*. And what we earlier called the public realm is now expanded into a public learning realm.

This 'instructive city' makes our surroundings as a whole subservient to the development of everyone by consistently giving priority to the goal of learning.

We can regard the city as a large school in which is embedded all the knowledge and understanding that has made a community what it is and with all the links and energies to best fulfil any ambitions present. As long as its size keeps it legible, its inhabitants and visitors can generally find their way around well enough and are familiar with the relevant addresses and signals. A city mirrors the world you are essentially familiar with and you know where there are things to learn or acquire as well as where not to go.

The more you take on board, the more you can handle. Children grow up in a reasonably easy-to-read world they can naturally make their own. Once that world grows bigger, however, detachment and alienation sets in. Then you have to keep control over an ever-expanding field of attention, which is a learning process. Nor does that field expand only in terms of surface area but also in depth. You also have to get at what is behind what you are seeing on the surface. We should therefore make everything in such a way that it is more explicit, explaining itself instead of holding back. If things are to become familiar they must make it quite clear why they are as they are and how they got that way. This is to prevent their history being erased, for the simple reason that things get replaced by others that are newer, better, bigger. For it is history that makes clear why things are as they are and what role they once played and that their form was not arrived at at random. History also makes us aware that things keep

The steps of Columbia University
(see pp. 234-235) as an area intervening between public street and
building, were originally intended
to keep the building at a distance
and give the city additional
freedom of movement.

changing, why this is so and whether this really is an improvement. Meaning is stored in the elements constituting the city, in their bricks, their architecture and in the place they occupy. These together, along with writings, images and music comprise a collective memory that contributes to a collective awareness and so will ultimately lead to social cohesion. Feelings, occurrences and people are retained and preserved as memories not just in monuments but in places, random objects, buildings or parts of buildings. The Learning City is in fact all about articulating these memories and making them transmissible and able to be read as the map of a community's memory. All those who shape the city have to realize before anything else that it could all be much more transparent and easier to get at.

A city becomes instructive by giving visibility to its past, its current situation and its intentions, to show what it has going for it. Whether visitor or resident, young or old, you should be able to read its history past and present and the achievements and values that obtain there now or have done in the past, noting their presence, becoming aware of them, familiarizing yourself with them. It concerns the widest imaginable range of potentials, experiences, associations and social contacts.

If learning to bridge the differences between people and between groups is increasingly an issue inside schools (alongside reading, writing and arithmetic), it should certainly obtain outside them when fitting out the public domain. By this is meant not just more play space and sports fields; the way schools are steadily transforming into a conglomerate of places should be extended into the public domain. Public space should be more than a traffic flow area. Social coherence can only be heightened by enhancing the capacity of social space. Not decreasing but increasing the number of places encouraging social relations can do much to diminish antisocial behaviour. Regrettably, modern cities have a lot less to offer here than most older ones which – and this must sound familiar by now – not only have more variety but are much more accommodating and hospitable.

► p. 251

# Tromostovje, bridges, Ljubljana, 1929-1932
## Jože Plečnik

Three bridges of the same provenance straddle the river Ljubljanica where it flows through the centre of the city of Ljubljana in Slovenia. These bridges link Prešeren Square with the old town from where you can ascend to the castle (Ljubljanski Grad), the highest point in Ljubljana, and look out over the entire city centre. Together constituting the true centre of the city, their explicit form is presided over by six prominent balustrades, given identical form with classicist motifs by Jože Plečnik. They present an image of unrivalled power and so visualize the identity of Ljubljana.

But why did Plečnik design three bridges instead of one? What on earth gave him this idea?! Formerly there was just one, which became too narrow to let pedestrians use it as the flow of vehicular traffic swelled. Instead of widened this bridge, which would have been the accepted solution, Plečnik added a new one on either side. By unifying the design he managed to edit the three into one, or rather a trinity. The original bridge is for vehicular traffic and the two new ones are for pedestrians only, leaving them more square-like than bridge-like and in a sense a prolongation of Prešeren Square. In fact, the square with this constraining structure hogging all the attention is simply extended to the other side of the river. It is not only the unity of the ensemble that is remarkable; so is the fact that with the original bridge now seconded by its new neighbours, the temporal layers of how it used to be and how it is today are juxtaposed. Maybe if the first bridge had been maintained in its original form, the past might have been stronger still and at all events more literally present. However, 'modernizing' the bridge and harmonizing it with the newly added elements has given rise to a composition that is perhaps more convincing and certainly more surprising due to the strength of the concept and the idea obviously underlying it. What is most important about this unique ensemble of bridges is the new significance it gives the city, in the sense that the city writes its own history and gains greater prominence as a result.

[1]

[2]

[3] Pieter Saenredam (1597-1665), *Interior of the Catharinakerk at Utrecht*, undated

[4] Antony de Lorme, Sint Laurenskerk, Rotterdam, 1657 (detail)

## Seventeenth-century church interiors

These days churches are closed except for briefly on Sundays. But it used to be otherwise, if a great many 17th-century paintings are to be believed. The church then was more a part of the street, as is still occasionally the case in more southern climes. In Barcelona Cathedral the public street actually runs through the church taking in a wide variety of religious presentations in the side chapels. Paintings show that even in the more northerly Holland a constantly accessible church space was no exception. This is where daily life was enacted little different from that in the street, none of which seems to have had a negative effect on the religious devotion. There you walked on paving partly consisting of tombstones of local citizens, and perhaps there was music as someone practiced the organ to the inevitable barking of dogs. There was something going on at every pillar. Children, dogs, beggars and tradesfolk populated these consecrated if unheated spaces,

exceptionally well-lit by the exceedingly tall vertical windows, not the mystical half-light through stained glass of cathedrals. The stone floors were all too often opened up to dig a grave, the way Public Works today always have some street broken open somewhere. Seen thus, the church seems an interior continuation of the street, sheltered against the rain and sun and without traffic (the same as in mosques, which are themselves often used for profane purposes and comparable with more literal roofed streets such as arcades). So it is ideal as a shelter, a meeting place and somewhere for children to play.

The most famous illustrations of church interiors such as those by Saenredam, usually eschew such busy scenes in favour of more serene, almost empty spaces. It is likely that this is grounded in an abstraction, the way architectural photographers seek the serene perspective, and that workaday

reality was reflected in the informal, industrious scenes illustrated by the more realistic painters. So the figures in the more populated paintings of Saenredam are better construed as furnishing and were presumably added later by others. For the record, art historians seem unable to resist interpreting the activities of figures in paintings as religious moralistic messages which they feel are to heighten the exclusiveness of these pictures rather than illustrate the richness of daily life.

We see here that a building with an explicit duty to perform lends itself to multiple use (as with the temples on Bali[10]) and so has much more to offer than was originally intended. This makes it an example of space with an increased significance. If space is made less exclusive and placed in a wider context, a more inclusive environment can emerge.

10  See page 231

[3]

[4]

# Street cubes, Amsterdam

Increasingly, we are confronted with more and more steel bollards and other obstacles in an endless variety of shapes and sizes, often acting in lieu of pavements to keep cars from hogging the entire street but on occasion as marking only.

The most apposite, without question, are the simple concrete cubes that invite one to sit on them, though without the pretension of actually being a bench or a table. These inconsequential grey blocks act as a magnet for small groups and are also a target for street artists. Apart from the fact that they channel the traffic, the way buoys demarcate a channel on water, they make the street more suitable as a locus for pedestrians and thus more conducive for staying, having in places the ambience of a living room.

[1]

[2]

[3]

# Monument for the popular hero, Amsterdam

You can find them in every city, statues of heroes from the past, heroes who managed to save, enrich or enlarge the city or country through their exceptional courage, intelligence or strength. On the whole these statues are larger than life, set high up on a pedestal so that you can look up at them from a distance, and often astride a horse in full gallop. The most eminent sculptors of the day were commissioned to portray these heroes, which gave them not only their magnum opus but also a share of the fame and publicity.

André Hazes, a popular singer about everyday life with many sing-along songs to his name, has been honoured by a life-size statue. Actually it is more like a cast of Hazes, microphone in hand, atop a stool at the very hub of the Albert Cuyp market, at home amongst his audience. The statue (or rather depiction) has no artistic value whatsoever, nor does it pretend to. It is simply the most literal rendition of the popular hero as etched in the public memory. It is regularly bedecked with flowers, often in large bunches, and constantly provided with cans of beer, of which Hazes was inordinately fond in life. There is always an audience looking on in admiration and respect, photographing or being photographed with their arm round their hero, as if a wish long cherished in life was now being fulfilled. That hero was one of them and will remain so as long as his songs continue to resound. The statue expresses this sentiment; even the greatest conductor or opera singer, whose fame extends a great deal further, could never emulate the honour bestowed on the heroes of popular culture. Of course, their fame is ultimately borne by the audio equipment that recorded their achievements and is to carry these forward, but it is just such a place that confirms and perpetuates the memory of the person behind those achievements.

Incidentally, there are many celebrities revered in the Netherlands that are sculpturally rendered as inconspicuous creatures. Modesty, here regarded as the greatest good, is borne out by a minimum presence. Putting people on a pedestal is foreign to our egalitarian culture.

One example is the author and educator Theo Thijssen, sitting in the street on an old-fashioned desk at which the prototypical Dutch schoolboy in his book of the same name (Kees de Jongen) is at work. This is putting the hero on a par with those passing by.

[4]

[5]

## Bijlmer Monument, 1994-1998
## Architectuurstudio Herman Hertzberger in association with Georges Descombes, landscape architect

The primary focus of this monument, made in response to the disaster caused by an aircraft crashing into a block of flats, killing forty people, was a mosaic carpet round a tree that had miraculously survived the disaster and was spontaneously adopted as a place of mourning and commemoration. The mosaic carpet, an idea by Akelei Hertzberger, was composed under her supervision and in collaboration with Jolanda van der Graaf executed by everyone caught up in some way with the disaster, members of the victims' families and neighbours who had survived as well as professionals called to the scene.

Close on 2000 mosaics were made in a workshop specially set up for this purpose, set in concrete tiles provided with standard openings of different sizes. Within the overall framework of this designed pattern everyone had their own place to fill with their feelings. Thus, everyone could contribute personally to this collective 'carpet'. Unlike a conventional monument where the event is commemorated symbolically by an artist representing those concerned, this mosaic carpet is a collective work of direct emotional utterances by those affected by the disaster.

It assimilates personal and shared experiences at the actual scene of the disaster, transforming it into a place of collective involvement and effort. This investment of personal concern teaches others what took place there, the way plants flowering in a garden reflect the love put into it. This place preserves the feelings of all those who worked on the monument, confirming it as a collective gesture.

[1]

[2]

A  At the centre of my tile is the anti-riot squad truncheon. They used this to beat on my front door during the night of the disaster. My doorbell was out of action and so they beat on the door to warn me that gas and electricity had been turned off. The blue and white stones are my front door being hit by the black truncheon. Left, the conflagration I could see out of my flat. Below that, the grey mass into which the block of flats, the plane and the people had been changed. I saw this grey pile the next morning when I went to see where the plane had crashed.
Below the front door the patch of grass between my block of flats and the site of the disaster. Above the front door the grey sky on that fateful evening.

B  a crying eye

C  In my tile I want to show that the fire station tunnel where we used to play football was not only a source of pleasure.
Two of my footballer friends died in the disaster, that's why there's a cross in the middle.
The red sides are the flames in which they died. I'm sorry I didn't get to know them better. I call them friends all the same, since they were always very good to me.

PS. Wherever they are, I hope they can keep on playing football.

D  A key,
A house,
A home,
A pot,
A plate,
A mug,
Life, living together,
Bang
– Broken pieces –
A past.

E  While I was working on it I felt hot and cold at the same time... Actually it's impossible to describe how I felt at that moment. On the one hand upset, and on the other happy that I could make something that will be there for centuries, in memory of my children Guillermo and Graciella, who were at home alone when the plane crashed... I made a mosaic in the shape of a heart for my daughter, she was so loving towards others... For my son I wanted to make a different kind of mosaic. It shows a track with a red and a blue car racing car. My son always tried to get the best out of himself, he had so many plans... Don't ask where I got the strength, but I'm glad I did it, it gives me a feeling of satisfaction. I was able to bring something to a conclusion...

F A key indicates life,
People living in a house.
Instead of shards, there are keys, nuts and coins, also a keyhole and a large fossil. A friend gave me that fossil, for me it stands for eternity, it's millions of years old. That screw stands for the engine's coach bolts. It's absurd that they bought the wrong bolts to cut costs.
The main thing about the mosaic carpet is that it reminds people how the commemoration of the plane crash forged a bond between the diverse ethnic groups.

G My tile is black with a red bar in it. I did this because I get emotional whenever I see the outpourings of grief among the enormously handsome Ghanaians with their red headbands, their music and singing. It is intensely moving to see them supporting and comforting each other in their grief.

H ... Enfin, j'ai décidé de venir pour faire une mozaïque. Les souvenirs de cette place sont bien avec hassan et aussi mauvais à propos de l'accident. Jusqu'à ce jour-là je ne sais pas mon ami est mort ou il est encore en vie. ...

## Outdoor books

At times you can still see books being sold in the open air at markets or in front of large book shops.

In the 1960s, it wasn't unusual for newspapers, magazines and books to be displayed out of doors, to be taken and paid for by leaving your money at the right place. This condition of trust has not exactly increased since then. All the more surprising, then, to see headstrong booksellers, undeterred, arranging daily displays of cut-price books outside their premises. These are almost defiantly accommodating places where you can make interesting finds (in this case on Saphartipark in Amsterdam).

[1]

[2]

[3] (photo Maurice Boyer)

## The Anne Frank tree

The hugh chestnut tree dominating the courtyard behind the Anne Frank House on Prinsengracht in Amsterdam is slowly dying and needs to be cut down. This far-reaching plan met with fierce resistance. Hadn't Anne Frank described this tree on several occasions in her world-famous diary, looking out on it from her hiding place? By being a part of that celebrated book, this tree has become part of the intellectual property of its readers and more than just a simple object. It has become irreplaceable, as the author's feelings and those of countless readers have taken up residence there. As long as the diary continues to be read and manages to affect its readers, this tree, through the attention paid to it by Anne Frank, like the secret annex, allows us to get closer to the author's feelings. It has become an item of common cultural property that cannot simply be chopped down. Maybe Anne's tree will live on as a sapling grown from grafts taken from it.

## Art in the park

The few parks in the centre of Amsterdam
are among the most intensively used public
clearings in this densely populated part of
town. They are filled to bursting point in
summer and winter, not just with people
looking for sun or some green space but
also with dogs being walked, street people,
children of all ages looking for a place to
play football, run and play in the sandpits
and at the table tennis tables – in short,
anything that the streets have no place for.
At a large open space in Oosterpark, it
proved possible on summer evenings to
directly relay operas being performed at the
city opera house onto a large screen in the
park. Thousands of visitors poured in from
all sides leaving no square metre of sitting
space unoccupied to be able to experience
these unprecedented, exclusive and usually
prohibitively expensive or sold-out events.
Even the many small children there with
their family at these unique occasions were
not left unmoved by the dramatic adventures of Wotan and Brünhilde.
Parks, as the largest public spaces not dis-
rupted by traffic, are pre-eminently suitable
for occasional large-scale cultural events. As
these can be communicated to all gathered
there, parks make excellent learning spaces.

[4]

[5]

## sesc Pompéia, São Paulo, 1977-1986
## Lina Bo Bardi

It would be impossible not to mention in the context of the Learning City the sesc (Serviço Social do Comércio), a 'cultural factory for the city'. This model scheme for leisure activities is an island which holds out better prospects for daily life in the impoverished metropolis of São Paulo. This perspective is underlined by the fact that the sesc is housed in a complex of old factory buildings where steel barrels were once produced. Just this reuse of old factory sheds, rather than erecting a gleaming new architectural statement as with so many sociocultural centres, makes the cultural activities taking place here easier to associate with work. So it remains a factory where

stuff is produced, no longer consumer goods but intellectual property for the spiritual development of the mainly deprived and underprivileged in a deprived metropolis.

You could regard the entire complex as a large leisure-time school with a theatre seating 1200, a library, studios for ceramics, painting, graphic art, woodwork, photography and weaving, a printing shop and a vast exhibition space. There is also a restaurant plus bar and a large 'living-space' with a fireplace and indoor pond. The extensive sports facilities with swimming pool are stacked in special towers added in the open corner of the site, their Elementarist and Brutalist

design sustaining the idea of 'architectura povera' in the new-build. Almost all the facilities assembled here, and the resulting contact between their users, are simply not found at most schools so that this complex does a good job of pointing out all the things that regular education lacks.

What we have here is an easy-to-read city set amidst an immeasurably large and inhospitable metropolis. sesc is like a big house where you are welcome and where there are forms of society sadly lacking in this metropolis – and all this in an explicitly instructive setting.

[1]

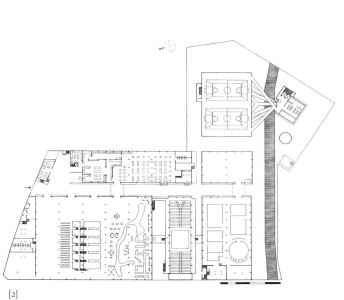

[2]

[3]

[4]

# A lesson from Christo and Jeanne-Claude

There are no other artists alive today who time and again succeed in temporarily transforming public space as the Christos do with large-scale spectacular events, this way reaching out and drawing everyone into their actions.

Even those who have now seen enough of such Christo themes as wrapping large urban objects such as buildings and trees, would have to admit that no other artist has ever succeeded in continually opening people's eyes to the unique aspects of the space they live in by temporarily altering the city. This is their way of increasing everyone's awareness, something artists today can do.

Nor is it just the technical side of accomplishing these projects that is full of risks. To get the authorities to actually agree to such a project signifies an almost unimaginable breach in the impenetrable fortress of laws, rules and practical objections of the fearful bureaucratic system that has us all in its grip. Here the artist is fulfilling an exceptional public duty, if only by showing that it is possible to escape these rules and regulations through art.

[1] *Wrapped Trees*, Berower Park, Riehen, Switzerland, 1997-1998 (photo Wolfgang Volz)

[2] *The Gates*, Central Park, New York City, 1979-2005

[3] *Wrapped Reichstag*, Berlin, 1971-1995 (photo Wolfgang Volz)

[4] Photo Joost van den Broek

[1]

[2]

[3]

## Sandberg's Stedelijk Museum, Amsterdam

When Willem Sandberg took over as director of Amsterdam's Stedelijk Museum in 1945, besides introducing art lessons for children there he did his utmost to make the inward-looking 19th-century building more visually accessible, as this would arouse people's curiosity about what they could expect to find inside and induce them to buy a ticket. When he had the opportunity some years later to add an extension (the Sandberg Wing, in fact designed by and accountable to the municipal authorities[11]) he insisted that the side giving onto the shopping street should be graced with large display windows, allowing passers-by to look in to get an idea of what was 'on sale' there. It was Sandberg's firm conviction that art is for everyone and that the museum should do everything it can to draw everyone in. Sixty years on, this is now standard practice and the popularity of museums has

more than borne out the efforts made back then to liberate art from its elite position. The Centre Pompidou in Paris had much to do with this. Sandberg in fact sat on the jury that chose Piano and Rogers' design. In 2006, when the Sandberg Wing (nothing special architecturally) was to be demolished to accommodate a major new enlargement, the then Amsterdam councillor for culture threw a first brick through Sandberg's windows as a symbolic gesture. This was the climax of festivities celebrating the start of operations and rang out the previous dynasty of innovation to a chorus of cheers. It must be assumed that the interim director responsible for this abject idea and the brick-slinging councillor has no malicious intentions and it was sheer stupidity that drove them to this deplorable 'symbolic' act.

However stunning the new building may

turn out to be, the incident remains significant and holds out little hope for continuing Sandberg's passion for engaging the street with what he had to offer inside. There is equally little hope for the future of the art education Sandberg so sought to stimulate and in which he was emulated in many museums throughout the world.

11 The 'Sandberg Wing', opened in 1954, was designed by J. Sargentini and J. Leupen of Amsterdam Public Works in association with F.A. Eschauzier.

[4]

## Art education

When children find the doors of the museum, the concert hall and the theatre open to them from an early age, they learn that these buildings are meant for them too. Lessons on art are just as worthwhile as, say, history lessons; they show you the way forward. Should you be denied these directions in the world of the imagination, it will not automatically become part of your own familiar world and you will for ever be distanced from the buildings where it all takes place: "For others perhaps, but not for me".

Lessons in art show you another side of things, show you that things are not fixed, that there are other possibilities and angles new to you. They see to it that all your senses are able to take in more. You are surprised, irritated, despairing, moved, thrown off balance and provoked into taking up a stance of your own. You learn to make distinctions, recognize differences and simi-larities, put things in perspective, see other ideas, underlying factors and relations and even perhaps gain an awareness of what beauty may be. Being confronted with your imagination can broaden your field of vision more than anything else can. You learn about other times, other places, about ephemeral and lasting values. In other words you learn that things can continually take on new guises.

Art will always have an element of exclusive-ness. It serves as an example but it isn't something you can simply consign to the street. Nor is there any need to as long as museums, concert halls and theatres are not exclusive bastions but a natural continu-ation of the street and the city. This was the very lesson Sandberg wanted his museum to teach.

[1]

[2]

[3]

[4]

[5]

[6]

## [The Learning City (continued)]

The modernization process invariably requires that fine-grained and fine-meshed networks become coarser and afford less variation. Even more serious perhaps than the units becoming enlarged is that the in-between space is simultaneously widened; after all, if a thing becomes larger it automatically has more space around it. When public space is enlarged, social life there becomes sparser and more detached. So public space keeps getting emptier.

Take the streets of many so-called underdeveloped countries where they still ply their trades in small businesses, the way we did in the Middle Ages. Anything left of this in our own cities is systematically driven out by legislation firmly rooted in environmental rules and regulations that regard everything as a form of pollution. Scaling-up, inevitable as this is, brings detachment and alienation in its wake. Processes our society depends on are unfolding outside our field of vision and without us being involved.

The paradigm of the Learning City asks architects and planners to pause at every design decision and seriously consider whether it has an alienating effect or incites learning. Learning and alienation are polar opposites. Learning is a process of identification and admission into a domain of your own. You become thoroughly familiar with your surroundings and make them part of your world. This brings certainty, giving you control over your surroundings and a place in the world.

Alienation is the opposite in all respects. Wherever we make the city (in other words, wherever it doesn't make itself) we must always be aware that we are then in an educational context, that is, one not exclusively about conveying information but about the challenge to get involved, this being the only process that can ultimately lead to appropriation.

A city is a Learning City when it asks questions as well as giving answers. Which brings us to a sensitive issue, for whenever we insist on safety, order and quiet, certainty is the major factor. And then multiplicity is soon supplanted by singularity. Because people want to know what to expect and keep tabs on everything, there is no room for doubt, there can be no uncertainties. Surrounded by a hermetic net of fearful craving for certainty, we need to find the holes so as to be able to undermine the established truths, tenacious as these are.

Anything that is defined, and its meaning established, has lost its space. It is the unallocated, unsignified and therefore freely interpretable element we call space that challenges us to get involved, appeals to us personally. We can only learn more by doing our own exploring. Learning is making things your own, in other words annexing them to your mental space.

Let's not smooth out the folds and let's see to it that the city doesn't lose its room to move, its space for play. It is precisely that which is *not* hermetically fixed and is still open to interpretation that makes the city instructive. The Learning City has to arouse one's curiosity and there must always be things left to be discovered. Everything must retain its space.

The 'city as a macro-school', then, is a call for another city, closer to a 'school as a micro-city', which is its micro-model; a school more oriented to discovery and thinking for yourself than to amassing information, a school more on the lookout for new possibilities than for the familiar. Our paradigm of the Learning City takes the mental development of all ages as a yardstick for designing the spatial environment. So making the city as instructive as can be should be the key spatial condition for urban planners and architects; this is what they should be focusing on.

This spatial condition is all about leaving space and making space for ambiguity, room to move and freedom of interpretation, allowing a more sophisticated, layered image of society to emerge. This is quite unlike uncritically helping to refine and confirm half-truths on behalf of a fearful population in search of peace and quiet.

[1]

[1, 2]  Classes in a cave, China 2007
(photos Reuters)

A Learning City shows its layers, thereby generating space for thought. Pushed through to its logical conclusion, it becomes what every school should be: an optimistic model of the world, whose occupants practise living together and try to get to grips with the whys and wherefores of everything around them. The school is a small world. The city is an enlarged version of that small world.

[2]

# Biography of Herman Hertzberger

1932 born in Amsterdam;

1958 graduates from Delft Polytechnic (today's TU Delft);

1965-1969 teaches at Amsterdam Academy of Architecture;

1970-1999 professor by special appointment at the TU Delft;

1982-1993 visiting professor at the Université de Genève, Switzerland;

1990-1995 dean of the Berlage Institute, International Postgraduate Laboratory of Architecture, Amsterdam. He was in addition visiting professor at universities and architecture schools in Argentina, Austria, Belgium, Brazil, Croatia, Denmark, France, Germany, Greece, Ireland, Israel, Italy, Japan, Mexico, the Netherlands, Slovenia, South Korea, Spain, Switzerland, Taiwan, the UK and the USA.

During his study and in conjunction with it Herman Hertzberger began on his own work and in 1960 founded an architectural practice, the Architectuurstudio HH of today. Famous buildings his office has produced include the headquarters of the Centraal Beheer insurance company in Apeldoorn, Vredenburg Music Centre in Utrecht and the Ministry of Social Welfare and Employment in The Hague. The practice is well-known for its many cultural buildings, schools and housing complexes, not just in the Netherlands but also abroad. Hertzberger has won a great many competitions, has been made an honorary member of several cultural bodies and has received national and international architecture awards both for individual projects and for his work as a whole.

From 1959 to 1963 Herman Hertzberger co-edited FORUM magazine together with Aldo van Eyck, Jacob Bakema and others. Hertzberger's projects have been published and exhibited all over the world. Along with many magazine articles he published two books, *Lessons for Students in Architecture* (1991), a compilation of his lectures at Delft University of Technology, also published in Dutch, Japanese, German, Italian, Portuguese, Chinese and Greek, and *Space and the Architect: Lessons in Architecture 2* (2000), a description of the contexts and ideas informing his work. Other recent books about his work are *Articulations* (2002), *Shelter for culture: Herman Hertzberger & Apeldoorn* (2004), *The theatres of Herman Hertzberger* (2005), *Dubbeltoren Waternet* (2006) and *Hertzberger's Amsterdam* (2007).

For further information and a complete CV and list of publications go to www.hertzberger.nl

# Bibliography

'1933. Groupe scolaire, Villejuif, André Lurçat archi-
tecte', *L'Architecture d'Aujourd'hui*, 370, May/June
2007, pp. 54-59

'1935. École en plein air, Suresnes, France, Eugène
Beaudouin et Marcel Lods architectes', *L'Architecture d'Aujourd'hui*, 370, May/June 2007, pp. 60-67

'Alison et Peter Smithson', *L'Architecture d'Aujourd'hui*,
344, January/February 2003

Bachelard, G., *La poétique de l'espace*, Paris: Presses
Universitaires de France, 1957

Bergen, M. van den and P. Vollaard, *Hinder en ontklonte-
ring: Architectuur en maatschappij in het werk van Frank
van Klingeren*, Rotterdam: 010 Publishers, 2003

Berlage, H.P., W.M. Dudok et al. (eds), *Moderne Bouw-
kunst in Nederland, Scholen I*, no. 13, W.L. & J. Brusse,
Rotterdam 1932

Berlage, H.P., W.M. Dudok et al. (eds), *Moderne Bouw-
kunst in Nederland, Scholen II*, no. 14, W.L. & J. Brusse,
Rotterdam 1933

Boersma, T., T. Verstegen et al. (eds), *Nederland naar
school: Twee eeuwen bouwen voor een veranderend
onderwijs*, Rotterdam: NAi Publishers, 1996

Bouw, C. and L. Karsten, *Stadskinderen: Verschillende
generaties over de dagelijkse strijd om ruimte*,
Amsterdam: Aksant, 2004

Broekhuizen, D., *Openluchtscholen in Nederland:
Architectuur, onderwijs en gezondheidszorg 1905-2005*,
Rotterdam: 010 Publishers, 2005

Brödner, E. and I. Kroeker, *Schulbauten*, Munich:
Verlag Hermann Rinn, 1951

Carvalho Ferraz, M., *Lina Bo Bardi*, Instituto Lina Bo e
P. M. Bardi, São Paulo, Milan: Edizioni Charta, 1994

Doumanis, O., *Takis Ch. Zenetos 1926-1977*, Athens:
Architecture in Greece Press, 1978

Duiker, J. 'Een gezonde school voor het gezonde
kind', *de 8 en Opbouw*, 3, 1932, pp. 88-92.

Dudek, M., *Schools and Kindergartens: A design manual*,
Basle: Birkhäuser Verlag, 2007

FORUM *voor architectuur en daarmee verbonden kunsten*,
VII, Amsterdam 1957

FORUM *voor architectuur en daarmee verbonden kunsten*,
XXII – 5, Duiker 1, November 1971

Geist, J.F., K. Kürvers and D. Rausch, *Hans Scharoun:
Chronik zu Leben und Werk*, Berlin: Akademie der
Künste, 1993

Gleiss, M., J. Fessmann and B. Stock, 'Hans Scharoun,
Bauten, Entwürfe, Texte', *Schriftenreihe der Akade-
mie der Künste*, Band 10, Berlin: Akademie der
Künste, 1974/1993

Goffman, E., *Behavior in Public Places: Notes on the Social
Organization of Gatherings*, New York: The Free
Press, 1963

Graaf, J. van der, A. Hertzberger et al. (eds), *Het verhaal van
tweeduizend mozaïeken, een monument*, Amsterdam 1996

*Harvard Educational Review*, Architecture and
Education, vol. 39, no. 4, 1969

Hertzberger, H., 'Huiswerk voor meer herbergzame
vorm' / 'Homework for more hospitable form',
FORUM *voor architectuur en daarmee verbonden
kunsten*, XXIV – 2, 1973

Hertzberger, H., *Ruimte maken, ruimte laten: Lessen in
architectuur*, Rotterdam: 010 Publishers, 1996. Originally published in English as *Lessons for Students in
Architecture*, Rotterdam: 010 Publishers, 1991

Hertzberger, H., *De ruimte van de architect: Lessen in
architectuur 2*, Rotterdam: 010 Publishers, 1999.
Translated as *Space and the Architect: Lessons in
Architecture 2*, Rotterdam: 010 Publishers, 2000

Hübner, P. *Kinder bauen ihre Schule, Evangelische Gesamtschule Gelsenkirchen*, Stuttgart: Axel Menges, 2005

Illich, I.D., *Deschooling Society*, Open Forum, London:
Calder & Boyars, 1971

Janofske, E., *Architektur-Räume: Idee und Gestalt bei Hans
Scharoun*, Braunschweig/Wiesbaden: Friedr. Vieweg
& Sohn Verlagsgesellschaft, 1984

*Journal Mural mai 68, citations receuillies par Julien Besançon*,
Paris: Claude Tchou éditeur, 1968

Karsten, L., *Oases in het beton: Aandachtspunten voor een
jeugdvriendelijke openbare ruimte*, Assen: Van Gorcum,
2002

Kurz, D. and A. Wakefield, *Schulhausbau: Der Stand der
Dinge, der Schweizer Beitrag im internationalen Kontext*,
Basle: Birkhäuser Verlag, 2004

Lagae, J., M. Stuhlmacher et al. (eds), *Oase*, no. 72, 'Terug
naar school', Rotterdam: NAi Publishers, 2007

Leeuw-Marcar, A., *Willem Sandberg, portret van een
kunstenaar*, Amsterdam: Meulenhoff, 1981

Marcuse, H., *One-Dimensional Man: The Ideology of Industrial Society*, London: Sphere Books, 1964

Mindlin, H.E., *Modern Architecture in Brazil*, Rio de
Janeiro: Colibris Editora, 1956

Montessori, Maria, *De Methode: De Ontdekking van het
Kind*, Bussum: Paul Brand, 1973

Müller, T. and R. Schneider, *Montessori. Lehrmaterialien
1913-1935, Möbel und Architektur*, Munich: Prestel
Verlag, 2002

Papalexopoulos, D. and E. Kalafati, *Takis Zenetos: Visioni
digitali, architetture costruite*, Rome: Edil Stampa, 2006

Paulle, B., *Anxiety and Intimidation in the Bronx and the
Bijlmer: An ethnographic comparison of two schools*,
Amsterdam: Dutch University Press, 2005

Rohmer, M., *Bouwen voor de next generation*, Rotterdam:
NAi Publishers, 2007

Roth, A., *La Nouvelle Architecture*, Zurich: Editions
Dr. H. Girsberger, 1940

Roth, A. *The New School*, Zurich: Girsberger, 1950

*Schools without walls: Profiles of significant schools*,
Educational Facilities Laboratories, 1978

Smithson, A. and P., *The Charged Void: Architecture*,
New York: The Monacelli Press, 2001

'Thema: Rückschau 1964, FU Berlin', *Bauwelt*, 34,
September 2005

Wilson, A., 'Forme et programme: le cas des écoles
anglaises de l'après-guerre', *L'Architecture
d'Aujourd'hui*, 339, March/April 2002, pp. 90-97

Woods, S., 'Free University, Berlin', *World Architecture
2*, London: Studio Vista, 1965

# Credits

This publication has been made possible by the generous support of the Netherlands Architecture Fund.

*Texts and compilation*
Herman Hertzberger

*Final editing of original Dutch text*
Vibeke Gieskes

*Translation into English*
John Kirkpatrick

*Image editing*
Eva de Bruijn

*Research*
Jop Voorn

*Editorial support*
Pia Elia

*Design*
Piet Gerards Ontwerpers, Amsterdam
(Piet Gerards & Maud van Rossum)

*Lithography and printing*
Die Keure, Brugge

© 2008 Herman Hertzberger / 010 Publishers, Rotterdam (www.010publishers.nl)

*English edition*
ISBN 978 90 6450 644 4

*Dutch edition 2008*
Ruimte en leren, 010 Publishers
ISBN 978 90 6450 645 1